NEW KIDS IN TOWN

ORAL HISTORIES
OF IMMIGRANT TEENS

NEW KIDS IN TOWN

ORAL HISTORIES OF IMMIGRANT TEENS

Formerly titled, *New Kids on the Block*

JANET BODE
20604

SCHOLASTIC INC.
New York Toronto London Auckland Sydney

Map by Joe Le Monnier

Originally published by Franklin Watts, Inc., under the title *New Kids on the Block: Oral Histories of Immigrant Teens.*

ISBN 0-590-29150-5 (meets NASTA specifications)

1 2 3 4 5 6 7 8 9 10   40   00 99 98 97 96 95 94 93

Printed in the U.S.A.

First Scholastic printing, September 1991

This book would not have been possible without the support and assistance of my family, my friends, and my advisers. Special praise goes to:

My sisters, Barbara and Carolyn, and my stepmother, Charlotte, for long-distance support.

My partner, Stan Mack, for editorial assistance and hand-holding.

My East Coast friends: Linda Broessel, Wendy Caplin, Chas Carner, Andrea Eagan, Neil Hedin, Marvin Mazor, Rosemarie Mazor, Sheryl Miller, Vince Pravata.

My West Coast friends: Lucy Cefalu, Carole Mayedo, Cindy Mitzel, Mike Sexton, Terry Thomas.

The students and staff at John Bowne High School, Flushing, New York, and especially Patricia Kobetts, the principal; Jean Stern, Inga Oppenheimer, Nancy Chu, the librarians; Linda Kiperman, an ESL (English as a Second Language) teacher.

The students and staff at Curtis High School, Staten Island, New York, and especially Karen Levy, the librarian.

The students and staff at Dr. Sun Yat Sen I.S. 131, New York, New York, and especially Dr. Archer Wah Dong, the principal; and Ernie Brill, an English teacher.

Martha Mendez, Executive Secretary, Bronx Venture Corp., Bronx, New York.

To my father
and fellow author,
Carl Bode

Contents

NEW KIDS IN TOWN

ORAL HISTORIES
OF IMMIGRANT TEENS

New Kids in Town

*Immigrant: a person who comes to a
country to take up permanent residence*

I live and work in New York City. Most mornings I start
my day by buying a newspaper at the store on the
corner. The woman behind the counter is an immigrant
from the Soviet Union. Walking by the diner, the sta-
tionery store, the market, the restaurant, and the deli, I
pass a United Nations of recent immigrants to this
country: Greeks, Hondurans, Haitians, Koreans, Chinese, Israelis. The chicken carry-out restaurant across
the street has employees who were born in six different
countries. The face of the city is changing.

When I have a chance, I visit schools to talk to
students about my life and theirs, about writing books
and growing up in America. Looking around the class-
rooms, I realize that the face of the whole country is
changing. In the public schools in San Francisco, California, for example, about one third of all the students
have immigrated within the last five years.[1] In New

York City, about one quarter of all students come from families headed by an immigrant.[2]

We are a nation of immigrants with a national make-up that's forever shifting. We continue to be the American Dream, the land of opportunity. In the mid-1800s when my German ancestors set sail for America, they were taking the same gamble that brings people here today. Then, nearly all immigrants were from northern and western Europe.[3] Now only 5 percent come from that part of the world.[4]

Then, if you wanted to come here, you came. But today immigration is more difficult. Over the last hundred-plus years, laws have been passed and extended and changed and amended.[5] Now once again Congress is debating the issue of who should be allowed in and who should be left out. And to this day, some of our residents—some of the children and grandchildren of yesterday's immigrants—want to close the borders to our future arrivals.[6] Once inside, some people develop a kind of collective amnesia, forgetting their own immigrant roots. We forget that our country's power and beauty stems from the very fact that we are a collection of different cultures.

———

I began to wonder: Who are today's immigrants, our newest neighbors? How are we different and how are we the same? What are we learning from each other? Because I realized I knew few of the basics, I set out to do what I like to do: ask questions. "Where do you come from? Why did you leave? Where are you heading in life?"

The answers are the heart of this book.

I talked with a handsome Nigerian who arrived here seven years ago a scared little kid and ended up the captain of his high school football team. And I spoke with a sixteen-year-old who hid the fact that he was Iranian. In a self-styled retaliation for Americans held hostage, his fellow students had taken to beating him up. I also talked with a girl from Santiago, Chile, below the equator where the seasons are reversed, who flew from summer to winter in nine hours. There was an Ethiopian, now described by friends as a "cool dude with a surfer ponytail," who fled his country after his father was abducted, tortured, and killed. I saw Irish brothers, sixteen and seventeen, who, despite fears of deportation, were on their own looking for work by day and studying for the GED by night.

And finally there was this thoughtful and driven guy from the Bronx, New York. He told me that until he went to kindergarten when he was five, he spoke only Spanish, the language of his homeland. What was unusual about that? He wasn't from a foreign country; he was born in Puerto Rico, a commonwealth of the United States. Still, day after day, he fought most of the battles that immigrants fight.

Many of the students I talked to had entered this country illegally. All of them had left relatives behind. Some escaped from war-ravaged nations; others departed impoverished lands. Still others came hoping for futures they believed were impossible in the place of their birth. Few of them really had any choice in the matter. Adults made the decision to emigrate and so they, the children, moved too.

Not all nations from which immigrants come could be included in these pages. As a starting point, though,

NORWAY

SWEDEN

FINLAND

DEN.
GER. POL.
CZ.
AUS. HUN.
ITALY ROM.
YUGO. BUL.
ALB.
GREECE TURKEY
TUNISIA
LEB. SYR.
ISR. IRAQ
JOR.
KUWAIT
QATAR
LIBYA EGYPT SAUDI
ARABIA
NIGER CHAD SUDAN P.D.R. YEM. OMAN
U.A.E.
DJIBOUTI YEMEN ARAB
REPUBLIC
GERIA CENT. AFR. REP. ETHIOPIA
CAM CONGO UGD. SOMALIA
GABON ZAIRE KENYA
RWD.
BUR. TANZANIA
ANGOLA
ZAMBIA
MOZ.
ZIM. MADAGASCAR
BOTSW.
NAMIBIA
SOUTH AFRICA

UNION OF SOVIET SOCIALIST REPUBLICS

MONGOLIA

IRAN AFGHAN. CHINA N. KOREA JAPAN

S. KOREA

PAKISTAN NEPAL BHUTAN
BANG. LAOS TAIWAN
INDIA BURMA
THAI. VIETNAM PHILIPPINES
CAM.

MALAYSIA

INDONESIA PAPUA NEW GUINEA

AUSTRALIA

NEW ZEALAND

THE NEW KIDS IN TOWN

Abdul-AFGHANISTAN

Francia-EL SALVADOR

Amitabh-INDIA

Jorge-CUBA

Emilio-PHILIPPINES

Martha-DOMINICAN REPUBLIC

Xiaojun-CHINA

Tito-MEXICO

Sook-SOUTH KOREA

Anna-GREECE

Von-VIETNAM

I called the Immigration and Naturalization Service in Washington, D.C., to find out the top ten countries for legal immigrants in the most recent year available.[7] The answer—Mexico, the Philippines, China, India, Korea, Vietnam, Cuba, the Dominican Republic, Jamaica, and Haiti. I asked about refugees, people who were living outside their native countries and were unwilling or unable to return because of fear of persecution. That top ten included Afghanistan, the Soviet Union, Laos, Ethiopia, and Iran.[8]

While deciding that in general I'd focus on teenagers from those countries, I knew that, of course, no single person could represent an entire land. What life was like growing up in a poor, Sikh household in Calcutta, population nine million on the east coast of India, was going to be different from life in a middle-class, Hindu home in the west coast city of Bhaunagar, population three hundred thousand.

I made choices.

On the following pages you'll read about the lives of some of these new kids in town. Yes, each immigrant's experiences were unique, but themes began to appear. All of them had endured a first day of school in a country where most often they didn't know the language. Some didn't even know the alphabet. All had been ridiculed and humiliated and sworn at by American-born teens. Words of hate entered their vocabularies: Cambo, FOB, Beaner. And all were culture-shocked, marked by a past that they couldn't forget and upon which their future would be built.

I learned from their stories—about the world beyond our borders, about how foreigners view America, and how these new arrivals are being treated in their adopted land. Often I'd open my atlas to find where exactly their journeys had taken them: where was Kuwait? Was the Republic of the Philippines really near Borneo? And I began to notice that as I read my daily newspaper, faces that hadn't been there before leapt from behind the headlines. When a reporter wrote of heavy guerrilla activity in Kandahar, Afghanistan, I "saw" Abdul. His mother, he had mentioned to me, wanted to return this fall for one last visit with her dying mother. An account of Vietnamese boat people being refused refuge by an American navy ship made me think of my new friend, Von.

———

For those of you who are immigrants, maybe parts of these stories will remind you of your own experiences. Maybe you will feel a little less alone realizing that what you're going through has been shared by others in the past and will be shared by even newer immigrants in the future.

For those born in the United States, maybe you'll gain a perspective on the global village that lies beyond your own tight circle of friends. Maybe you will come to understand that our nation is richer because it is a rainbow of cultures and different points of view.

The words that you will read were originally spoken in the immigrant teens' own voices. At times the sentence construction might seem a little awkward. The grammar won't always be perfect. But as much as possible, I wanted you to hear their stories as they told them to me. There is one difference: to protect their privacy and their safety, I changed their names and some of the facts of their lives. The basic histories, though, the emotions, and the sense of the experiences are absolutely real.

Abdul
AGE 17, AFGHAN

I don't date. My religion forbids it.
My marriage will be arranged.

Afghanistan is a landlocked Asian nation of bleak deserts, jagged mountain peaks, and the famed Khyber Pass. Surrounded by the Soviet Union, Pakistan, Iran, and a sliver of China, this Muslim country has been vulnerable to its neighbors for thousands of years. In the fourth century B.C., Alexander the Great stormed across it on his way to India. The seventh century A.D. saw Islamic conquerors; the thirteenth, Genghis Khan. During the next centuries, Afghanistan was a battleground, then an independent nation and a kingdom ruled by an emir. In 1979, with Soviet troops rumored to be entering Afghanistan, Abdul's father decided that for his family's safety and future, they must leave the country. In 1989, after a war that created more than three million Afghan refugees, the Soviet troops withdrew. Today Abdul, who lives in Brooklyn, New York, thinks back to the land of his birth and worries about his homeland's future.

Suddenly at four in the morning my father and mother said, "Wake up. Be quiet! Hurry!" My brothers and sisters, we were very surprised. "Where are we going? Where are we going?" we said.

"We have to leave now," my mother said, and she helped us get dressed. I was very scared. I was just a little boy, seven years old. But I remember well. The smugglers, their trucks, the desert. I remember small things: I couldn't decide what to take and what not to take. My soccer ball? My science book? My mother said, "Don't take anything."

My father was always listening to the radio. He was very curious about the world. I think he suspected the Soviets were going to attack and he was scared. I didn't talk to any of my friends about this. It was just in my house with my family that we talked about the Soviets and that maybe we should go out of Afghanistan. Nobody else knew. It was our family secret.

In the darkness we waited for a car that would take us to the smugglers and their truck. By the time we met them the sun had come up and it was early morning.

There were three smugglers. These men live in the desert. That is their place. They were smuggling other things, too, but I don't know what. That was covered and under our feet and those of the two other families who were heading out. We were hiding in the back of the small truck, standing but with our heads down so you couldn't see us. The smugglers were driving very fast. We were bouncing around, almost falling down. They were scared of the Afghan, the Pakistan, and the Iranian governments, that we would be caught up by one of them.

I had no idea where we were going. I thought we were going to die. We didn't know what was going to happen next. We were out there and there was nothing! Flat desert full of sand. Very hot. No food. No water. No other people. Suddenly we heard a noise; it sounded like a plane. The smugglers said, "Lie down! Lie down on the floor of the truck!" We lay down and my father and mother said, "Don't cry, children. It will be all right." The sound disappeared and again silence, only the sound of the truck.

At night it got very cold. We had a little food from my house, but soon that food was finished. We were drinking salt water that was mixed with oil. The smugglers did that on purpose. They didn't want us to drink too much, because there wasn't any more water in the desert. My parents and those guys tried to calm us. Each hour, they were telling us, "Nearby, there's a city. There's a lake. There's a lot of water." It was their way of telling us, "Be strong. Don't get sick. Don't die."

The second day we met a shepherd. We were very lucky. The smugglers bought a sheep from him and killed it. We all ate together. It was my last night in Afghanistan. By the light of the next day we crossed into Iran, to a town called Zahedan. We were safe. The smugglers took ten thousand Afghani money from my father for this trip. That's a lot of money, like a thousand dollars. Then we went to a motel where we stayed and rested for two or three days. Zahedan is not a good place to live because it's too near the border. Instead, we moved to Shiraz, a big city in Iran to live with relatives.

I was very sad to leave Afghanistan. I liked my life there in Kandahar. It is the second largest city after

Kabul, the capital. There were no apartment buildings in Kandahar. We had our own house; it was big with all the rooms around a central courtyard, like having a backyard inside. But we all slept in one room, me, my parents, my four brothers, and two sisters. Afghan people don't like living in different rooms. They have large families and like to be together. My uncle lived on the other side of the house with his family. My father owned a small shop. My mother stayed home. Most women don't work in Afghanistan. My brothers and sisters and I went to the local school. I played outside with my friends. The weather was warm; we were near the desert. We didn't have snow the way they did in Kabul, to the north in the middle of many high mountains.

———

Two months after we came to Iran, my father heard the news: the Soviets had invaded Afghanistan. He had been right. "Now," he said, "it is time to enroll in school." For one week, two weeks, we went to school, but the teacher would say, "You need an Iranian birth certificate." We didn't have that. We were in the country illegally. My father was very worried. I thought the only scary part was leaving my country, and now it was scary again. The school found out we were Afghan and we were thrown out. My father said, "You must find a job in order to have a future. Staying at home doesn't help."

I was a plumber's helper to a friend of my father's. I worked with pipes. He'd tell me what to do. He didn't pay much because I was just there to learn how to become a plumber. My brothers became tailors. My father worked in a shop. My sisters stayed home with my mother.

We were in Iran for six years. One day my father told us we were going to the United States to go to school, to have a future. There was no future for us in Iran. We didn't even have legal papers. And so, once again, we left. We had to go back to Zahedan, then we went south, illegally again, to Pakistan. There we would find an American Embassy.

———

The day we arrived my father went to the embassy and tried to get us here as refugees. We knew that the United States takes people to come here. We didn't know there would be a very long line wanting to go. When my father's turn came, they told him, "Come back to the embassy office with all your family, not just you." It was very hot there in Pakistan. We lived in a building with other people who waited in line. Days passed. Weeks passed. My father worried. Would we get to the United States? Would my sister we left in Iran be okay? Would his other children be okay? He got sick. I don't know what happened. In his sleep, he died. A heart attack?

For us, there was no turning back. We must go to the United States. We couldn't go back to Afghanistan because there was war. We didn't want to go back to Iran because we had no papers, and if we returned, our friends would say, "What a shame." America was our only future.

By then, it had been a few months, we had everything, all the papers. But when my father died, we had to go tell the embassy. They didn't believe that it was true. They thought it was a trick! They wanted proof of his death. Finally, finally, they accepted our papers; we got the airplane tickets and we came.

After school I watch TV—"Three's Company"
and "Different Strokes"—to help me know
what's going on in American families.

I was fourteen then. Within a month of arriving, I enrolled in a big public high school. I remember I was happy that I was coming to school again to learn something, to become someone. But I was scared, too. The school counselor just looked at me and said, "If you're fourteen, you're in the eighth grade." Getting used to studying after six years was hard. I had to learn English because my family didn't speak it and we couldn't talk to anyone.

One period a day they put me in ESL, English as a Second Language. The words began to become a little familiar to my ears. But the American kids gave me a hard time. They made fun of me. And the curse words! All day. Every day. If the teacher asked me a question and I knew the answer, when I said it, because I couldn't pronounce it well and I had the wrong accent, they laughed at me. I felt very bad.

I couldn't do anything about it. Even if I had wanted to get physical, fight with them, it wasn't good. I'm not an animal. I'm a human being. I have a brain. I can talk. Why fight? Being peaceful, I think, is the best way. Some teachers knew what was going on, but they didn't care. I was a problem they didn't need.

I wanted to go back to Afghanistan. I hated this place. I didn't have any friends. I didn't have anyone to talk to. I still don't have a lot of friends, good friends, like best friends. My sister and brothers went to a different school. I was lonely, but I had to deal with it. I went through it. I went to school. I came home. And I had to study hard to learn English. Like in social studies I had to read, then I'd find a word where I didn't know the meaning and I had to look it up in the dictionary. It would take me a long time to do just one page.

———

Now I'm seventeen and the American kids don't always know that I'm a foreigner. They tease less. I found out that if you act the way they do, say the things they say, do the things they do, they will be calm. So I try not to act strange to them. I wear T-shirts and stone-washed jeans and aviator glasses. My hair looks like their hair. I'm about five feet ten inches. Clint Eastwood and Charles Bronson are my heroes. After school I watch TV—"Three's Company" and "Different Strokes"—to help me know what's going on in American families, what they do.

There are no others from Afghanistan in my school. Afghan people are spread all around. You can't find them too much. In each city you can find one or two. That's it. Sometimes I tell people where I'm from and I'm very surprised that they don't know Afghanistan. They are very weak in geography. They say, "Where's Afghanistan? Is it a town? Do they have cars? Do they have school?"

I always think about my country, going there one day, seeing it, practicing my religion with no problem. Religion is very important in my life. I am Muslim. We have a small mosque where we go on Saturdays. From eleven to three I go to religious school. I study Dari and Pashto, the two languages of my country. Then from eight to midnight, I go to mosque. I believe in Allah and his Prophet Muhammad. The Qur'an is the holy book.

There are rules, the Islamic rules, for everything, for daily life. But here I can't practice my religion when I should. Five times a day I should pray, the first time before sunrise. I can do that with my family, but at school I can't say to my teacher, "Please, teacher, I need to leave because I must pray." Also the food in school is a problem. I'm not allowed to eat all kinds of food; pork, for example. I just eat pizza because of the cheese, that's all right. Other things I don't eat, because I don't know how they make it. Or it's not right, the way it should be for a Muslim. So I do without.

I don't date. My religion forbids it. My marriage will be arranged. For a Muslim, your parents have to decide who you should marry. For me, my mother and my uncle will discuss it and decide. Then they will say, "This girl is good for this son." That's fine with me. In fact, I think it's perfect. I know my mother; she went through it herself and she knows. I don't have to think about disease. I know I'm going to marry someday, so why should I date girls? I listen to my mother. I don't want to change my culture and forget my language.

———

For me, for all Muslims, it's very unusual to be here. A Muslim woman should cover herself with what we call a chadoor. It is a long, black robe that covers everything, her body, her hair, her face. They have little holes for the eyes. My sister doesn't wear one. She says, "Here, other people don't, so I don't. People would laugh if I do that." My mother still wears her chadoor and in the home, too. I'm not supposed to talk to girls at certain times. I make a sin if I look at a lady without the chadoor. Looking at people who go to the beach, in their underwear, that's a sin for me. Other immigrants from different cultures who come here get used to the American habits. They date girls. They do what Americans do. But not so much us.

———

Ten years from now I hope to be married, have a career, a house, and children. I will raise them to be good Muslims. They are my face of the future.

Francia

AGE 15, SALVADORAN

*Some people were what we call
"disappeared." They had been
captured and taken away, maybe
by a death squad, gangs of men
that frighten and kill people.*

Francia was born in San Salvador, the capital of the small Central American country El Salvador. A Pacific-coast nation, it borders Guatemala and Honduras. For more than half of her life, the people of El Salvador have been locked in a grim civil war. The sides: the U.S.-backed ruling government and its army with links to extreme right-wing death squads versus the left-wing guerrillas. In less than a decade, an estimated 70,000 have died and 500,000 have fled to the United States. Most Salvadorans enter illegally, including Francia and her family. This pint-sized ninth-grader talks about her life and the day she learned she would finally be joining her parents in America.

I remember that day—always. My brother, Guillermo—that's William, Willie, in Spanish—and I were in school. I was doing equations in math when the principal came into the room. "Francia," she said, "your uncle is here. He says you have something important to do." I went, "Uncle, what's wrong?!" And he goes, "You're going to have a surprise. You are going to travel in one month to the United States to live once more with your mother and father."

Oh my, we were so happy! We were jumping. We were running. We were doing this and that. My parents sent money so my uncle could buy us some new clothes and pay for the man to bring us here. Many people from my country who travel to America suffer a lot. Some even die. My father and my mother trusted this man. They told him to take care of us. They also told him we would travel with this lady, my uncle's girlfriend. My father was trying to make a family again, like before.

Getting ready to leave made me remember the day so long ago, I was only nine then, when my father told me he was going to America by himself. He took Willie and me to school. He said we had to obey our mother and be nice kids. We said good-bye. It was very sad. He came in illegally, but I don't know how he did it. He never talks about it.

Many things were happening in my country. I was very little, though, and couldn't understand it all. Some people were what they call "disappeared." They had been captured and taken away, maybe by a death squad, gangs of men that frighten and kill people. Everybody thinks that maybe the army and the police have done that. But the army says it's the guerrillas that take them to make them fight against the army.

The man next door taught school. One day some men came to his family house and told him and his family to stand in the street in front of it. The father, you could hear him saying, "Take anything; just please don't hurt us." The men shot the father. The mother and the children watched. Then the men took from the house and left. The next day the neighbors were gone.

With my father, it's not that he got in trouble. But the police were looking for a man, and they confused my father with this guy. Because of the situation in my country, my father knew there could be trouble. They might put him in jail, or worse. The life was very hard. Prices were higher and higher. People couldn't find work. My father wanted a better life for all of us.

El Salvador is a wonderful country. I feel sad for all these problems. My father worked in a place where they kill the beef—a slaughterhouse. Since he was a little boy, my grandfather, his father, taught him how to do that. That was my grandfather's work, too. My mother was a cook.

After my father went to America, my mother took us to live with her mother. She lived in a little town. Maybe a thousand people lived there, not as many as students in this high school. It was hilly and there were other little towns on the other sides of the hills. The people who lived in these towns planted and grew corn and wheat and every kind of fruit—mangoes, papayas, oranges. When those foods and fruits were ready to eat, they took [them] and sold them.

A year after my father left, he wrote to my mother, "I have saved money from my job. I want you to come live with me." My mother told me and Willie she had to go. They would save two times as much money so we could also travel to the United States. Again it was sad saying good-bye, this time to my mother. Each month my mother and father sent my grandmother money for the food, the clothes, the books for school. We lived with her in a big, big house, and my other uncle and his wife lived there, too. Out in the yard were the animals, so many chickens and ducks and turkeys and dogs. Every week my cousin Myra would come visit; she was my same age. We used to go in the back where there were the trees and very big rocks, and along with Willie, we'd play soldiers there. If we walked a little, we came to a river where my aunt would go to wash the clothes. We used to go swimming there. It was such a nice place.

I didn't think to feel frightened. Everything we needed, my grandmother gave us. Sometimes my parents would call. We had no telephone. We had to go to the public place where there were phones. After one year of living without my brother and me, my mother couldn't stand it. She missed us so much. She worked with a lawyer to try to get papers for us, but it was no good. We would have to travel illegally.

At the border, though, we had a problem. The guards said, "You are supposed to be with your parents if you want to come to Honduras. You can't pass."

This man, the one my parents paid money, and my uncle's girlfriend and Willie and me went in a car from my grandmother's house to the town of San Miguel. We stayed there for one day and then we went in a different car to Honduras. That's the country right next to El Salvador. At the border, though, we had a problem. The guards said, "You are supposed to be with your parents if you want to come to Honduras. You can't pass." Willie and I started crying. We cried and cried. The border guards still said no.

We're Christian people; we started praying. God helped us because this man who was helping us talked to the guards and they said, "Okay, fine, you may go." Maybe he gave them a little money when he talked to them, but I think it was God. So we drove and we drove on little dirt roads. They were bumpy and we never seemed to stop.

Willie was sitting on the girlfriend's lap and he kept saying, "I have to go to the bathroom! I have to go to the bathroom." Finally, he couldn't stand it no more and WHOOOSH. He got her all wet. The lady went, "Oh, my dress!" That's when this man stopped the car and said, "Okay, okay, go to the bathroom." Willie said, "What for? It's too late." My brother was so embarrassed. I was eleven by then, but he was only eight.

It felt like forever, but we did get to Tegucigalpa, the capital of Honduras, where the airport was. We stayed in a hotel for the night and the next morning we were supposed to take the airplane to Mexico, to Tijuana. But there was a problem with the engine. We had to wait one week until the next plane to Tijuana left. Finally, we got to Mexico and into another car to go to a hotel. That night this man's friend came to meet us. We were going to pass by car from Tijuana to the United States in the dark.

I was so scared, I was going, "Oh, oh, oh." At the

border, we were supposed to say something in English. I don't remember what it was because I didn't speak any English then. The man told Willie and me and the lady to practice. We kept practicing and practicing while we drove closer to the border. We met a boy. He got in the car, too, to go across with us. And then you know what happened? I fell asleep with my brother and woke up when we were in Los Angeles already! We went, "What? When did we get here? Are we okay?"

They said, "Everything's okay. You're going to stay in this house until your father gets here."

I was frightened and my brother, too. Other people were staying there. They were speaking Spanish, but I don't think they were from El Salvador. I really don't know who they were, maybe church people. Pretty soon we were on another airplane, this time to Dallas, and then I saw my father waiting for us behind a railing. I just ran and hugged him and said, "Oh, Father, I love you!" And I hugged him some more. We got home and my father was so happy he was playing jokes on my mother.

She said, "Where are the children? Where are the children?"

He went, "They didn't come today. They come tomorrow."

"Oh, you're such a liar."

"No, I'm serious," he said.

Then we couldn't stand it. We went, "Ma, Ma!" We were so excited. It had been two years since we had seen my father and one year for my mother.

Today my father has a job taking asbestos out of buildings. It's dangerous, but it pays good. Before that, he'd worked in a factory, then as a janitor. My mother has a job cleaning house. She cleans two houses a day. It's a lot. First she was working for a lady, but that wasn't fair. My mother would clean two houses for fifty dollars each. This lady did nothing but take my mother to these houses. For that she got all the money from the second house. Now my mother is getting the work on her own.

I'd have to say she works not because she wants to or because my father wants her to. She works because we need the money to send back to my country for the rest of the family. We are the only people who can help them. In my country, things are even worse than when we left: more expensive but no more jobs.

We live in a three-room apartment. My father and my mother live in one room. Willie has one and I have the other. I have my little bed in it, blue curtains, a brown rug, and a dresser with a big mirror. I put my perfume on it and my jewelry.

My parents say, "It's not too soon to start to think about the future. You have to decide what you want to do." I like health careers. Since I was a little girl, I want to be a physician's assistant. I talk to my friends about this, too. They're from all different countries: Colombia, Peru, Equador, Mexico, Guatemala. I like them very much, but my parents say, "First you have to think about yourself. You have to study. Try to pass your classes. Don't cut."

There are some friends in school that push me to do some things that I don't want to do. I tell myself, "I don't have to do it, if I don't want to." They go, "Here, do you want to smoke?" I'm not going to smoke because my friends do. I say to myself, "Do what you think is right, not what other people say." I think it's right to study a lot. "If you study a lot," my parents say, "someday you're going to be somebody in this world. It's difficult; everything is difficult. If you do your best, you're going to make it."

My mother and father want me to get a high position. "Now that you have the opportunity," they say, "you have to take it. Maybe it will never be in front of you again." They tell me also I have to take care of myself. They remind me of all these girls that get pregnant so early. "Be careful on that point," they say. "Everybody makes errors. Sometimes people do things without thinking of the consequences. Think first of what you're going to do, why, and what might happen." To make sure, they don't let me date yet. My father says, maybe if I study enough, I can go out in a year or two. What can I do but obey them?

We read the Bible together. We go to the Baptist church on Sundays. We also have meetings on Wednesday night at 7:30 P.M. and on Saturdays; the teenagers have meetings in the church at 4:30. The pastor is from Mexico; his wife is from Nicaragua. Everybody else is from El Salvador. It helps me so I don't feel completely cut off from my country. For my birthday, it was in April, the church gave me a big party. It was my fifteenth birthday. In my country, we celebrate the fifteenth as important, instead of the sixteenth. I got balloons and earrings and this barrette.

Sometimes I think I would like to go back to my country, see my family, my friends. Life is very different here. Before I came, my mother sent me beautiful pictures from the United States. There were flowers and everything. So when I was in my country, I thought everything here must be beautiful and clean. When you are in a foreign country, everybody thinks being here must be like heaven. But that's not what it is. There is something different about this country. It's hard to describe.

One of the things I like about here is that you can get more things. Like Willie wanted a bicycle. In my country he couldn't get it. Here, he did. My mother has eight pairs of shoes. In my country, she only had one. But what I don't like is that it's such a dangerous country. Well, not in all parts, but where I live there are drugs and gangs and stuff. In my country I didn't even know what drugs meant. In my country people are still innocent until they are like fifteen years old. My little brother, he knows so many things and he's only nine. When I was nine years old, I knew almost nothing about life. I just knew how to go to school, how to eat, how to play.

In my country, I think there is more freedom—no, that's not the word I mean. In some ways it is. In some ways it isn't. In El Salvador you may go to this person's house and that person's house and the people are so nice. You know them and they know you. They won't hurt you like they might in this country. In this country you can't trust anybody, because you don't know what this person wants from you. That's some of the difference between this country and that country. I wish both countries could always be safe for the people.

Amitabh
AGE 15, INDIAN

*Tea was spilling all over
the place. I was crying.
My mother was telling us,
"Pray. Pray."*

India is a sprawling nation, a peninsula with the Ara-
bian Sea to the west, the Indian Ocean to the south,
and the Bay of Bengal to the east. Its other borders
touch six separate countries: Pakistan, China, Nepal,
Bhutan, Burma, and Bangladesh. Archaeologists have
found evidence of civilization dating back at least 4,500
years. India today reflects its past: the Dravidians, its
earliest known inhabitants; the Sanskrit-speaking
tribes; the Moguls; and the British, from whom it
gained independence in 1947. This densely populated
land is the birthplace of the Buddhist and Hindu religions, and the home of many others—Muslim, Christian, Sikh, and Jains. Five years ago, when Amitabh
was ten, he and his parents and two brothers moved
here from Bhaunagar. Now his American dream is a

career in the Air Force in aviation electronics. One day after his ROTC class, we met in his high school library. He recalled his first months after arriving in the Washington, D.C., suburbs.

————

It is really bad for us in the beginning. We were five in a two-room apartment. Every day my parents would get up and go out to look for jobs. They knew they had to start all the way at the bottom, that people here didn't count any experience from India. But my father had been a biologist. My mother was a chemistry professor at a university. In India they were both making good money.

Now, though, they would come home every evening and they wouldn't have found anything. They would be very, very sad. They didn't know the bus systems or the subway systems here. They'd get lost. They'd get to some place and it would be too late. The job would be gone. They'd go to another place and the answer would be, no. One day, my parents said, "This is a dead end. We can't find jobs. We don't have any more money. Nothing. We're going to have to jump into the river." I want to think that they were not being serious, but I still would feel so sad for them and so sad for us.

I couldn't always understand why we had come here. Why would they leave the country where they had been born, where their children had been born? Bhaunagar was a modernized city on the northwest side of India. It had a lot of factories, apartment houses, and private homes. Our home was three stories high and we lived together with my uncle, my aunt, and my grandparents. My grandparents had another house in a small city called Mehsana. Every summer and during other vacations, we'd go there.

The weather was very warm. In the winters it would get cool enough to wear sweaters, but that was it. No snow. It also used to rain quite a bit. There was a dry and a rainy season, with monsoons that occurred every year at a certain time. We had a good life there.

I know that people think that in India everybody is poor, that everything is backward. It's not that backward, and it's probably improved since I've been here. We had electricity and running water and traffic jams. I went to a good school. They taught the same subjects as over here, like art, general science, and math, and also some of the different languages of India. I think there are fifteen or sixteen languages. At home we spoke Gujarati, and I learned how to speak Hindi, too.

I was happy. I knew the way things were done in India. I knew we were Hindu. In that religion we had many, many gods, some that I didn't even know. We had a lot of religious festivals. We used to go to temple. We could go any time we wanted. We believed in "karma"; how we acted in past lives decides who we will be born in future lives. My family god was a god named Siva. It was a good god. He had many arms. He was very powerful and had snakes around him.

I knew the food. I loved cooked okra, the vegetable, and pouri, the bread. I had a favorite kind of curry. I knew my future. I knew that when I got married, I would bring my wife to live with my parents. The bride's family would provide a dowry, money and silverware and things like that.

My parents said, though, that we would move to America because us kids would have more opportunities for the future. This was a long time planning. I don't even remember the first time they told me. At first it went so slow. I did not know anything about America. Once, a friend of mine who was Christian took me to this place to get American hot dogs. At that time I had no idea what they were. I took a bite and I spit it out. It tasted disgusting!

But then sometimes I would get interested in coming here. I heard there were big buildings and fast cars. My older brother told me, "Over there in the United States you never see the sun. It's always snowing. When the sun does shine, it's a holiday." I thought like wow! About a month before we left, my parents said, "We're moving to America." That's how they told me. And I said, "Yes." I told my friends in school and they said, "Yeah, sure, sure." I said, "Really. Watch."

We took a train from our home in Bhaunagar to Bombay, a city, my father said, about the size of New York. Then we flew from Bombay to the country of Kuwait and then on to London, England. I'd never been on an airplane before, so I didn't know what to expect.

Just before we were supposed to land in London, the whole plane started shaking all over. People who were standing up fell. Tea was spilling all over the place. I was crying. My mother was telling us, "Pray. Pray." Luckily, everything became all right. There had been an air cap. It's some technical word, I don't know what it means. We landed and then flew to Kennedy Airport in New York City and then National Airport in Washington, D.C.

I had my first hamburger and said, "Forget it!" I threw it out.

After the first few months my parents found jobs, but the work was very tough on them. My father worked as a messenger, more a job for a boy than a man. He delivered letters and carried packages all over the city. Again, he would get lost the way he had when he was looking for work. He lasted about three or four months doing that until he found another job, and another job. All small jobs. Then he met an Indian man who owned a laboratory who hired him. Now he's sort of back in the area of biology, where he used to work.

My mother started working at a store. She had to fold clothes, mostly. Then she got a better job watching patients at a senior citizens' home. Eventually, she became the dietitian there. And now it's okay for me, too. Kids don't look at me strangely the way they did in the beginning. I had my first hamburger and said, "Forget it!" I threw it out. Eventually, though, I got used to it. Now I eat anything. I eat hot dogs, hamburgers, chicken, and french fries. I love pizza. In India I remember that once we had a fair and they had pizza, a small triangle, for eight rupees, about twenty-five cents. "It was better than the hot dog," I thought then.

Now we live in the suburbs in a big house with four bedrooms. I have my own bedroom with military posters all over the place. My middle brother and I have a computer. We have more than six hundred games for it. He wants to work in computers. My older brother is in college, the University of Maryland. He wants to be a surgeon.

I'm in the tenth grade. ROTC is my favorite class. I'm planning to go into the military right after I finish high school. It should help me out a lot because ROTC trains us for the military. Since when I was in India, my ambition was to make the military a career. I remember every time my father would take us to a shop, I'd want to buy military-colored clothes. Just yesterday I was looking at some photographs taken at my aunt and uncle's wedding in India. There I was, just a kid, in a military uniform. I don't know why I'm into it so much.

My parents don't mind, since I like it. I considered the Air Force Academy, but I talked to a recruiter who said I had to have at least a ninety average to make it. My average is seventy-five to eighty. What I have to do, though, right after school is out for the summer, is see how to be a citizen. If I join the Air Force without being a U.S. citizen, I'm offered jobs, but not as many as if I am a citizen. The job I want, aviation electronics, requires citizenship.

My father wants to become a citizen, too. My mother wants to stay Indian. Still, we are all changing. When we lived in Bhaunagar, my mother wore a sari. She used to put a bindi, that little dot, on her forehead. Now only when we go to some festival, like every August 15 is Indian Independence Day and there's a big parade, then she will wear her sari and have a bindi. Mostly, she wears pants and a blouse.

They keep up on the news, what's happening in India. Back when the prime minister, that's like the president, Indira Gandhi, was murdered by her Sikh bodyguards, we were all shocked. There were phone calls going around in the whole Indian community here. That was something that we never imagined would happen. I guess for us it was the same as when somebody tried to kill President Reagan. Except with Mrs. Gandhi, they succeeded.

I'm more Americanized than my parents. I still speak Gujarati at home, but now there's English mixed in a lot. I'm trying to get out of my accent as much as possible. And now I have what I guess you could call an American mouth: I have braces. I'd never seen braces in India. I hate wearing them!!! Just like American kids.

Jorge
AGE 16, CUBAN

*If I use drugs, I'm killing
my father and mother.*

Cuba is an island about ninety miles south of the tip of
Florida. After Columbus landed there in 1492, the
native Indians died off from diseases brought by his
sailors, or were killed by the settlers that followed. For
the next four centuries, Cuba was home for Spanish
explorers and immigrants, French and English pirates,
black slaves, and free laborers. By the dawn of the
twentieth century, Cuba had gained its independence
from Spain. Thirty-some years later, its then-leader,
Fulgencio Batista, turned the nation into a police state.
In 1959, Fidel Castro, a former student leader turned
lawyer, and a band of guerrillas forced Batista from
office. Castro then began programs of dramatic economic and social change. Land, banks, and industries
would come under government—not individual
owners'—control. Opponents of Castro and these programs were often imprisoned. Some were executed.

Cuban-born Jorge, an intense and handsome six-footer, starts his story with that of his father.

———

My father was a political prisoner. He spent nine years in jail in my country. His crime was he didn't like Castro. Sometimes my father talks about that time. It was very hard to be in Castro's jails. They treated the prisoners like animals.

The first thing my father did when he got out of jail was marry my mother. She waited for him all those many, long years. That's really love. The next thing he did was to try to come here, to America. But it wasn't possible. He couldn't get a visa. So he went to work cleaning the sewers, the job the government let him have. My father and mother lived in a small town near Havana, the capital, where they both grew up. And soon, I was born. Eight of us, all relatives, lived together in an old, one-floor house. I shared a bedroom with my grandmother, who I love with all my heart.

In Cuba, the government controls your life. Everything is rationed. Each family has a little booklet called a "libreta" with coupons in it. You want to buy a pair of pants? You can't just run over to K-Mart or Macy's or some shopping center. In Cuba, each family is assigned a special week to shop for clothes, say, May 21 to May 28, and K-Marts don't exist. You're supposed to go those days to get what the coupons say, maybe one skirt or one shirt. You get one pair of shoes for one year. Even underwear is rationed, three pairs for each person for one year. The same thing with toys.

Depending on how many people live in your house, you have a certain number of coupons for food, too. Your family is assigned to go to one particular store; that is the only one that accepts our coupons. When I am in Cuba my favorite food is rice and beans and roast pork. But it is hard to find pork. Any meat is hard to find. I don't even know there are such things as shrimp, clams, and lobsters, and Cuba is an island surrounded by shellfish. I only learned about these things once I come here.

You can't ever say, "Oh, this street is very old. They should fix it." That is antigovernment talk.

In school the teachers talk to you about Castro. Always. When you are in geography class or history class or any class, they say good things about him and bad things about the United States. For example, they don't say that there is AIDS in Cuba. They say that Americans put AIDS in Cuba. They teach you that Communism is good. Communism does this and that for the kids. And always they talk positive about Russia. Starting in seventh grade, you have to take Russian, like here you take Spanish or French.

And starting in seventh grade, all kids, male and female, have to go to a camp and work for the country. You don't get paid. It's considered service that you give. You go wherever they send you, sometimes very far away from your house. You are without your family for forty-five days. They can visit only one day, Sundays. You don't eat things that you eat at home. You sleep in very rough conditions. You go to the bathroom in out-houses. You work on government-run farms cutting sugar cane, planting, taking fruit from the trees. My father didn't like that I had to do that.

Everybody has to go in the military, too. When I lived there, they might send kids to Angola, in Africa, where there was a war going on and the Cuban army was involved. Or to Nicaragua where there is fighting, also. My father didn't want that to happen to me; the same thing for my mother.

In Cuba for your future, you can't study whatever you want. It's whatever they—Castro and the government—want. Maybe you say, "I want to be a lawyer."

They say, "Well, let's go check." They come back and tell you, "No, we have too many lawyers. You're going to be . . ." whatever they need, maybe an accountant.

I don't think they would ever give me a good career, anyway. You see, I am Catholic. In Cuba if you want to go to church, you have to go in private. I did my first communion and other stuff and had to be sneaky about it. People who go to church are not Communists, so they don't tell other people they are religious.

Castro feels that for the young people, religion should not be part of your life. He doesn't care about the old people. He knows they aren't going to do anything for Cuba. So he puts his attention into the young people. But still, old or young, you always have to think, is my neighbor watching me?

There is a special group that is called "comite," like committee. In each block they have a house and the people inside are supposed to watch you and what you do. They watch where you go, what time you leave, and when you return. They might even report it. If you got a lot of friends to your house, they're going to ask you, "Why have you got a lot of friends to your house?" If you have a lot of parties, "Why do you have a lot of parties?" You can't ever say, "Oh, this street is very old. They should fix it." That is antigovernment talk.

One day when I was thirteen, my father said, "We are going to Venezuela." I started to cry because I knew I was going to leave my grandmother, and my aunt and uncle, too. I was going to leave my friends and the only life I ever knew. Venezuela would be just a stopping point before coming here. The only way we could come to the United States was by way of a second country. My father told me, "I think that leaving Cuba is best for you, and best for all of us. But, if you don't want to, we'll talk some more and try to work something out."

I said, "No, Poppy"—I call my father Poppy—"I want to go because I don't want to stay here and do whatever Castro wants." But it was hard. In my little town everybody knows you and you know everybody. It's like family. That's part of the culture. Sure, some of them are with Castro and show to Castro that they love him. And, sure, all the neighbors knew that my father and mother didn't like Castro, and sometimes they gave us a hard time. But my mother was a loved lady because she helped others there. She was almost the mother of the whole neighborhood. "To be safe," my father said, "keep our leaving a secret."

On the way to the airport, I thought to myself, the worst thing that Castro does is to separate families like us. We left some of our family in Cuba and now we are here. In different ways, he kills families.

We went to Venezuela with a visa to stay there, not a tourist visa. Our plan was then to try to come to the United States. We tried and tried. For seven months we stayed with relatives. I didn't go to school. My father would go to the American embassy and try to get permission to come here. Finally, there wasn't any way to do that legally. My father decided we would come here illegally. He didn't tell me how we did that, but I know we had to go to Miami and say we came from Mexico or something like that.

———

Now, four years later, I'm still very close to my parents. They believe in what I do and they are sure that I'm not going to do anything wrong. I know some teenagers use drugs. I've never used drugs and I won't. If I use drugs, I'm killing my father and mother. I know especially American-born teenagers talk about wanting to be out of the house and independent. I don't feel that way. I believe that our parents gave us life, so we have to do whatever they want. And I know that what my parents want for me is always the best. They're not going to tell me to do something wrong. I love and respect them.

They're proud of me, too. Almost from the day I come here, I work. First I work forty-five to fifty hours a week in a restaurant owned by a family friend. Two months ago I start to work at a video store, thirty-five to forty hours a week now at four dollars an hour. I buy furniture for the house, for the living room, for my bedroom. I buy the TV, a ring for my father, a chain for my mother, a vacuum cleaner. I buy clothes for myself and jewelry. I open a bank account. I give my mother a trip to Disney World and Epcot Center.

That doesn't mean I forget about school. My average for the whole year is eighty-something. I wish it was better, but what can I do? I'm in school until 2:45 and I have to be at work at three o'clock. I work until 8:30, quarter to nine, around there. I work straight through. I don't eat dinner until I go home, around

9:30. My mother waits and we have dinner together. Then I do my homework for maybe an hour or two each night, and go to bed around eleven or twelve.

My father works in the restaurant where I used to work. He is there every day except Wednesday. My mother goes to clean the restaurant in the morning. Sometimes he helps her. He starts working at seven in the morning and stays until twelve at night. I'm awful worried. He's a little old and with a lot of problems with tension, stress, and high blood pressure. I'd like to help him, but my only day off is Sunday, so we can't talk that much.

On Sunday I sleep late, 9:30, and go to church. I go alone. The mass is in Spanish. I know other Cubans who go there, but they don't know me. Then I go home and maybe visit with my friends, buy records, go to a ballgame or to some place that my mother wants to go.

Sometimes I wish I had a little more time for myself, but then I think, "It's all right. Everybody has to sacrifice. In the future I will see the things that I might miss now. I will say, well, now is my time." My first dream is to be a great actor. I think, though, that all my doors are closed. I don't have a friend who can help me with that. I don't know how to get there. So if not, I want to be a lawyer, or, maybe, something else. I'm saving money so I can go to college. Or buy a car.

In my future, I dream that I have a good profession and I am married. I have children and I raise them with two languages; always Spanish in the house, English in the street. That's very important. I will tell them how Cuba was and how Cuba is. But I want you to know this: I feel good here in America. This is a very beautiful country. I'm not American, but I feel very proud of America. I think this is my adult mother. America.

Emilio
AGE 19, FILIPINO

My American friends want to go drinking.
My Philippine friends want to go dancing.
I'm trapped in between.

In 1521, the explorer Ferdinand Magellan paid a high price for being the first Westerner to discover what is now known as the Philippines. He was killed by the inhabitants. Within fifty years, however, the Spanish had claimed the archipelago of seven thousand islands as its own, named it in honor of its king, Philip II, and founded the city of Manila. Three hundred-plus years later, in 1899, following Spain's defeat in the Spanish-American War, the Philippines were turned over to the United States for twenty million dollars. Finally, on July 4, 1946, it achieved full independence.

Since then, this Pacific nation has seen several presidents, including Ferdinand Marcos (1965–86), who imposed martial law—rule by decree—and looted his own country's treasury. He was succeeded by Corazon Aquino, the widow of a man who had been assassinated for opposing Marcos. A decade ago, because Emilio's parents were anti-Marcos, they decided to emigrate to America with their six children. Emilio was eight. We first met at New York City's St. Patrick's Cathedral following a mass honoring Lorenzo Ruiz, the first Filipino saint. After spending half his life in this country, Emilio compares the two from a teenager's eye-view.

I've dated both Philippine and American girls. It doesn't matter, they all give me problems. But there are major differences. In Philippine families we believe in the double standard—even if it's mean. American girls can do things that Philippine girls could never do. I can't believe American fathers let them get away with what they get away with.

I live in Connecticut, and for a while I had a Philippine girlfriend who lived on Long Island. When we went to the junior prom, she wasn't allowed to stay over at my house, even though my mother was here. It was considered wrong. If my date had been an American girl, it would probably have been no big deal. She could stay out all night.

In a true Filipino family, the daughters can only go out when they are a "good age," and then a brother goes along. When I have a family, I'll be stricter with my girls than with my boys. My girls won't be able to date until they have finished college. Philippine boys can start dating when they feel like it.

My American friends want to go drinking. They take drinking seriously. My Philippine friends want to go dancing. I'm trapped in between. Sometimes I think I'm more Filipino because I'm really into dancing.

Also, I'm a DJ and have been for two years. It's my business and my hobby. I have business cards and my friends give me recommendations. I've bought my own equipment and do parties. Filipinos want nonstop dancing, no talking. I try to match up the songs so it sounds as if it's a single long one.

Other times, I think I'm American because my real goal is to have my own company—in any field. I want to own a Ferrari, be successful in life, have four or five kids, and maybe a few extra luxuries like a beach house.

In the Philippine culture everyone helps out. Neighbors like to help neighbors, and they don't expect anything in return, especially not money. If some family is moving, everyone helps. Of course, there has to be food on the table for nonstop eating. With some of my American friends, it seems that they can't do favors unless money is involved. It's money, money, money all the time.

When I walk in my house, it's both countries. I speak both languages at home: Visayan, the language we talk on my island, and English. When my mother scolds, she does it in Visayan. If I look around, I see a nice house with a fireplace. I never thought I'd have one of those. The living room and formal dining room have Japanese and Filipino furniture. The family room and kitchen are 100 percent American. In my bedroom on the walls, I have posters of fast cars and music groups.

———

I'm from Cebu, a small island south of Manila. When people ask me where it is, I tell them it's not far from Vietnam or Taiwan or Malaysia or Borneo. If that doesn't help, I just say it's on the other side of the world from America, across the international dateline, fourteen time zones away. There are many, many islands; my father was from Negros. They speak Visayan there, too. People on other islands, like the one where Manila is, speak Tagalog. Ilocano is another dialect. To know English is a big deal.

In the Philippines and on Cebu there are poor people, middle class, and rich. The poorer people live in the suburbs and the country. They are the ones selling barbecue corn by the side of the road on the highway. They grow rice and take it to an outside market to sell it. Sometimes I'd go with my mother or the maid to the market to buy fish. There are vendors in little stands where you buy it. I remember thinking that the fish smelled too much.

———

We had a comfortable life. Where we lived was considered middle class. No one was in hardship. We lived in a nice house and had the usual: a TV, telephone, one car, and one jeep. Both my parents worked. My father was an accountant and my mother was an English teacher. I was the baby of six children and everybody said I was spoiled.

I could get the maids to cook me anything I wanted. My favorite was a spicy sausage, chorizo. I really liked jackfruit, too. It was the size of a watermelon, tasted chewy, and had lots of juice. Having a servant in the Philippines was not a big luxury. The middle-class people often had a maid. The rich people had one maid for each kid.

Once we went to visit the family of one of our maids. They lived in the mountains where there was no electricity. Everything in their home was run by batteries. That maid took care of me while Mom was at work. My mom insisted I have a hot lunch every day, so the maid brought it to school. Spoiled, I know.

————

My parents were against Marcos and his government. That's why they wanted to leave. They wanted to get away from it all. I don't know all the details, because when I was around, my parents didn't talk politics. I remember a time when I was scared. I came home from school and found Mom and Dad running around like crazy. I had the impression it was about an election. I'm not sure. I grew up in the time of martial law, so it was always a little tense. During certain hours nobody was allowed outside at all. I don't remember exactly when, but maybe from midnight to 6:00 A.M. Once our two maids got caught out and we had to go to jail to pick them up.

In the Philippines, at least in Cebu when I was growing up, everyone dreamed of going to the United States. My friends and I looked up to the Americans. We didn't meet many of them, but when we thought of America, we thought good things and easy living. Sometimes my mom would tell me about World War II and the Philippines and the United States. She told me about MacArthur, an American general who she said came back to help us and won the war.

We came here in shifts because we had paper-work problems. First my father arrived by himself. Six months later I came with my mother and two brothers. Then the rest came six months after that. Everything seemed to be working out, but then my father died. My oldest brother really helped keep us together.

He's the main vein of the family. He inspires us. We

all promised that we would chip in and help. We all started doing our own laundry. We took turns with the cooking. My oldest brother promised to move the family to a safe neighborhood. Where we lived when we first got here was not good. Our car got vandalized three times in one month and a gang lived across the avenue.

Starting in seventh grade, I worked every summer. I went from gofer in a Japanese furniture store to a dishwasher in a restaurant. I only lasted two months at that. Then for two years I worked at Benetton's. That's when I started to get into style.

With the money I earned from my job and my discount, I began buying my own clothes. Pretty soon I branched out and now I like the designer Tommy Hilfiger and another one named Girbaud.

Still, my older brother has dates and I don't. He teases me. He says it doesn't seem to matter that I have a great flat top and look handsome behind my square-rimmed sunglasses. I'm beginning to think the only way I'm going to get the girls to fall for me is to go back to the Philippines and let the ones there know that I grew up in America. Some of them still think that is special.

Xiaojun, "Debbie"

AGE 13, CHINESE

*If the teachers didn't think
we were paying attention,
they took a stick and beat us.*

China has a wonderfully rich and dramatic history. Three thousand years of rule by a succession of dynasties was followed by a briefly interrupted six hundred years of rule by foreigners. It remained, however, culturally and technologically advanced. In fact, this Asian nation is the homeland of the oldest continuous civilization in the world. In 1949, under the leadership of Mao Zedong, its name became the People's Republic of China. Mao's drive to establish rural communes, to industrialize villages, and to eradicate the ways of the past brought success and, at times, national trauma. There were periods of mass executions and the forced relocation of millions of city-dwellers to rural areas. By the 1980s, this U.S.-sized country with four times our population—over a billion people—began to seek better ties with the non-communist world. Four years ago, when she was nine, Xiaojun immigrated to the United States. Accompanied by her two best friends, also immigrants from China, we interview Xiaojun at a public library near her home in New York City's Chinatown. Outside is the din of the traffic. Inside, Xiaojun, an effervescent eighth grader, describes her life in rural China.

———

We had a relative, a second uncle, who lived in the United States. He sent us a tape. We all sat in the living room, put it on a tape recorder, and listened. He said we should come to the United States. He told us to bring "lots of clothes because it's really cold, but no cups or plates because they have them. And bring a blanket."

I didn't know any history of America except someone had told me that everybody had a slave. I thought, great! I'd come here and get my very own slave. I would not have to carry water any more!

———

I'm my parents' oldest daughter. I have a younger brother and a younger sister. We lived in a small village in a house made of brick. It had a big room in the middle, and all the way in the back we could go up a ladder to the two bedrooms. We shared the house with my uncle and his family, ten of us all together. Sometimes my parents and my uncle and aunt would talk about their early life. My father and mother came from the city. He was an architect and built houses. I don't know why they all moved to the country. They didn't talk about that.

We had no running water in the house, but we

were lucky because we lived near the river. Every morning at 5 A.M. I would go and—pant, pant—get water. I used a big stick and carried the water in buckets balanced on it. The water we used for cooking and for bathing.

We slept on hard, wooden beds with no mattresses. There was no telephone, no television, no VCR. There was no "I want my MTV." The most we could get was a radio. We had electricity in the house, but used it only when my parents said we could. Usually we used candles.

There was a little houselike building with the cooking fire inside. We didn't have much wood, just sticks, so instead we used the stalks from the wheat. First we put them in the sun to dry or we boiled them with other things like carrots for feed for the pigs. We used every part of everything. Mostly my mother and I did the cooking. That was one of the duties of the oldest daughter. We ate mostly rice and vegetables, sometimes my favorite, bok choy. Only at New Year's would we have chicken and soup.

I had other chores. I had to clean the bathroom. Well, that is, it was a sort of bathroom. It was a bucket behind the bed or outside. (In big, big, big houses in the village, they have, like, latrines.) I had to change my brother's diapers. I had to help him take a bath and wash his hair. I had to take care of him and my sister after school. Sometimes I really got mad at them and yelled at them. In China the oldest starts cooking at five; you change diapers at six.

My mother, she was the oldest daughter in her family, too, had to feed the chickens, collect the eggs, and clean the coop. She and I helped tend the village's pigs. We had a garden; everybody did. And everybody worked on the village farm. Together we grew wheat and rice and other stuff; I forget what.

The weather and the crops were very important. If the weather got bad, oh, oh, we were in trouble. We worried and worried. When it was harvest time, we had to cut this and cut that. The adults were so busy they can't even stop to make lunch for the littlest kids.

We helped our families and we went to school. In China our parents were turning us over to the teachers to educate. They could use the same punishment as our parents. That meant the teachers were strict. If we were late, we had to stand outside the door for one hour. If the teachers didn't think we were paying attention, they took a stick and beat us. Or they took a ruler and smacked our hand until it turned red and black and blue. They pulled our ears like they're stretching them. When we talked, monitors wrote our name on the blackboard, or they made us sit without a chair, on an invisible chair. It was really painful when we didn't do good at school, and this was just elementary school!

After school, I would visit and play with my girl-friends. There weren't any games, no toys, no swings. We didn't have bicycles; only my father did. But we did have lots of homework, even for little kids. At my house we would all sit around the table and my mother would help us.

There was a nice thing about school, though. That's where the one TV was. Whole families would go together to watch television, like you might go to the movies together here.

Religion? In my village there was a little Buddhism. I don't know much about it. I think they meditate. Some people knew kung fu. Some people knew how to look at your future. I believe in genies and mermaids. I pray at night to myself. I keep thinking, how were humans made? I don't know. I ask almost everybody I know. I look it up in the encyclopedia and I can't find out.

––––––

In the Chinese culture men are more important than women. If the parents die, the woman doesn't get anything. Only the men get the house, all the money, everything. Because my mom was the biggest sister, she had to do every job in the house. My father's the only son and he doesn't have to do that much. It's important to have a son. If the wife can't give birth to a son, the husband's mother will tell him to marry another.

With my mom, she saw only a picture of my dad. Her parents said, "You have to marry this man on such and such day." I don't know if they fell in love or not. But in China, that's the way most marriages happen. What's strange, though, while married people argue a lot, there's not much divorce.

In China you're not supposed to have more than one child. I have a brother and sister because it was before this rule. My mother's friend had a second child. She went up to the mountain and hid the baby. But the government found out. They killed her and the baby. At least, that is what my mother told me. They do that because there are too many people and not enough things to go around.

––––––

If you want to move from China, it is very difficult. A lot of people sneak out. My father sneaked out using the ID card of my second uncle. First you take a plane. When those people ask you where you are going, you don't say America. You say Thailand, or something like that. Then you go to one place, change planes, and fly to either Mexico or Canada. If you go to Mexico, you have to climb through the mountains at the border, show the fake ID, and say you are just traveling. If you go to Canada, you just drive across. They don't check you a lot. If you're caught, you're in big trouble. They can even put you behind bars.

After my father got here, he began to work and to send money home. My mom used some of it to get fake ID cards for us. Then one day she was piercing my ears and using ginger and oil to help them heal. "Your father wrote a letter," she said. "He's earned enough money and he got an apartment for us."

My friends were sad to see me go. I gave them all the things I had; my pencils in a pencil case that my uncle had bought for me in Hong Kong. I gave them my rulers and my books and all my clothes. We couldn't buy things as much. We don't have parties the way they do here. We just do weddings and New Year's. We don't know Mother's Day or Father's Day or Christmas. Everybody cried and said good-bye.

We brought our suitcases out to a car we had borrowed. I remember my mother was trying to fit them in. We took the car to a boat, to a bus, to a boat again, and on to another bus to a city. Then we got on a train. When the train stopped we had something to eat, and for the first time ever I had a soybean drink. It was really good. I wanted to save some to take with me to America, but my mom said no. Finally we got to Hong Kong for my first plane ride. The pilots gave me crayons and I thought they were something to eat. What did I know? I was just a little nine-year-old from the countryside.

———

It was real different in New York. It looked almost nothing like China. No foreigners ever came to my village. I had never seen a black person before. I'd never seen any Americans. My mother told me, "People kidnap and kill each other. You have to watch the window and the door all the time to make sure nobody comes in." I could hardly sleep.

The first night my parents prayed for good luck. They took strings and then put matches to them. And they prayed that I go to school and do well. I was very scared to go. The teacher said, "What's her name?" and my mom told him Xiaojun, my Chinese name. He said, "Does she have an English name? No? Well, what about Debbie?"

"Okay," said my mother and that's how I got my name.

"Marry a Chinese guy," my mom says. "All Chinese think the same." I don't agree, but I don't tell her. I think Americans must be the same as us inside."

Coming to America has changed my life. Now my parents work too much and too hard and I never see them. But we do have a TV, a radio, a microwave, and a washing machine. I still have things to do, like sweep and mop the floor, do the dishes, mop the table, clean the mirrors, wash the fans when they're dirty, wash the clothes in the washing machine, and take care of my brother. For this I get five dollars a week allowance.

I get up around 7:00 A.M. I leave for school between 7:30 and eight. School is over at three. I have to go straight home every day after class. I can't go out at night. They know where I am right this minute. Once I'm home I study for four hours. Before I eat dinner, my father gives me a little lecture. He says, "Work hard so when you grow up it will be easier to get a good job and make money. If you don't get a good education and a scholarship, you might have to beg for money. You don't want that."

My mother tells me, "Don't have any boyfriends. You can't date until you are twenty-two and then you can't be late coming home." I don't know if she's joking or not. But I do know they'd be going crazy if I came home with a boyfriend, and forget it if he is American. "Marry a Chinese guy," my mom says. "All Chinese think the same." I don't agree, but I don't tell her. I think Americans must be the same as us inside.

I'm a good Chinese daughter. I help my parents by looking up telephone numbers for them. Sometimes I have to call the electric company, read the advertisements for different things, take care of apartment bills. I do what they want.

I think of being a doctor, help people get healthier and make their lives easier. I also think about being a model, like Christie Brinkley, or maybe an actress or a lawyer or a cop or a singer. My parents say, "Be a secretary." They tell me, too, "Stay involved with our Chinese community," and I do. But, of course, I'm not an ABC, an American-born Chinese. The ABCs sometimes curse at us and call me and my friends FOBs, "fresh off the boat." I don't like that. I turn my eyes away.

———

I cry at night sometimes. My father says, "What are you doing?"

I say, "Nothing. Nothing." I get real confused. In China my father went with me to the school to watch movies on television. We had time together. I used to tell him my problems. Now there is no time. Here I can watch TV any time and I don't have to get the water or take care of the pigs. I guess I like it better in America.

Tito

AGE 14, MEXICAN

My social studies teacher says,
"Comics are too much fantasy."
I tell him, "I need a little fantasy
in my life."

Mexico, nearly five times the size of California, is our southern neighbor. Its people and history are a powerful mix of the native Indian cultures and the conquering Spaniards who originally came in search of gold. In 1524 the first Catholic priests arrived to convert the Indians to Christianity. For the next three hundred years, Spain ruled Mexico, until it won independence in 1821. This rugged nation has survived emperors and dictators. Today it grapples with an economic crisis and staggering rates of underemployment and joblessness. When Tito was four years old, his mother took him and his brothers from Tijuana, Mexico, to join their father, a naturalized U.S. citizen, in Los Angeles. Now, ten years later on an August afternoon, Tito sits in the living room of his family's three-bedroom home and talks about life in his neighborhood.

———

After a while, I got used to having drug dealers around. I just hoped they'd stick to their own areas and not approach me too often. But, of course, I'd have to say they are a problem. They are dangerous. Dealers are one more part of the life I have to accept. My parents don't like it, though they don't know what to do to change it. They talk to me about drugs. They aren't like some of my friends' parents who say, "I don't want to find out you're doing drugs. If I catch you with this or that . . ." In a way that makes you feel that they don't trust you.

"You can't ignore drugs," my parents tell me. "But it's dumb to use them. They only bring more problems." There are a few people that I know that are addicts to one drug or another. Myself, I've never tried any drugs. Always kids I know at school tell me, "Oh, you'll try them sooner or later."

The first two years after we emigrated, we lived with another Mexican family. When I was about six, we moved to this house, and now eight years later, even I've seen the neighborhood change. There used to be a big orange tree across the street on an open field. I love climbing trees. I'd climb that one, then lay back and eat my fill of fruit. The leaves gave me a nice, cool breeze. The shade, it was great.

I made up my own dream world. I was up in the stars, flying around and looking at all these different times. Maybe the stars were shining in the morning or the rainbow was upside down. Pegasus the flying horse, unicorns, ancient Indian gods, they were all in my world. It was a place to get away to. If I had a problem, I'd climb the tree and start thinking about all this. After that, I'd feel better. It was almost like meditating.

One day when I was twelve I heard shouts and trucks and equipment. I looked out the window. The orange tree was gone. Now dealers and gang members hang out in front of the apartment building that was built. I concentrate on life inside my house with my family, but sometimes it makes me feel like a caged bird.

My father works the night shift in the produce business. He loads the trucks with fruit and vegetables that go to the supermarkets, and he manages some of the other people who load them. My mother takes care of the house. She tells us it's important to eat dinner together, but usually we can't do it because my older brother, he's a junior, works from 4:00 P.M. until midnight. When he gets home, he always heads to the refrigerator for leftovers. We all know everything my mother cooks turns out good. My favorites are tamales and pisole. But her favorite is menudo, a soup with rice and pork skin in it.

I'm in the ninth grade now. The school is seventh through ninth. Last year I switched schools because the one I was attending was mostly American students. The teachers paid more attention to them. Where I go now, I think it's a good school, even though it has a bad reputation. What I like is that the teachers don't care what our culture is. They help us all.

After school, usually I go home because my parents worry if I spend too much time on the street. Until recently I couldn't go out unless I asked permission. And that's unusual because most of the guys my age, they want to go out, they say, "I'm going out. I'll be back at such and such an hour." It frustrated me. I would see kids a lot younger than me and they were outside. I didn't know what to do. But then again, I understand my parents are strict because they are only trying to protect me.

At home, I eat a little and then I watch TV, a lot, four or five hours. I can do my homework at the same time, that is until my mother catches me and makes me turn it off. There's a Mexican version of "60 Minutes" that I like, but I have to admit what I love are cartoons. My mother says, "You're too old for cartoons." But I love animation. I love to laugh. I read a lot of comic books, too. Spiderman is my favorite, and the X-Men, the Fantastic Four—the guy who stretches all over. My social studies teacher says, "Comics are too much fantasy." I tell him, "I need a little fantasy in my life."

My parents say, "You come from a different background, so to get ahead you have to do twice if not three times better than the American-born person."

When I grow up, I want to get married and have kids. I want to teach them who they are; what their heritage is. I want to give them a sense of belonging to some place. Every year my family visits the town near Guadalajara where my mother comes from. For me it's like going to a paradise. I am breathing fresh air. The people are friendly. It's not like big cities where it's so crowded that everybody has their own little circle around them. "Don't get too close!" they say with their eyes. In cities there are so many people around I don't know who's going to do what to who.

In my mother's hometown, you can say "Hi" to someone and they'll smile a big fat smile and say "Hi" back. Then it's, "Don't I know you? Aren't you Carlos's grandson? Yes? Oh, we're great friends. We used to go to school together."

My mother moved from that town to Tijuana when her father lost his bakery business. She was very brave and strong. She found a waitress job and sent her parents money. My pop came into the restaurant once and really liked her. He went there again and again and she started giving him special attention. Then they got married and had us three kids. For many years she didn't want to move to the United States because she didn't think it was a good place to raise us. Finally, she came and has had to struggle here, too, but she's always survived and done okay.

"Be proud that you're Mexican," my mother says. I know many people have a bad impression of Mexicans and Mexico. They think that all our money goes for beer and drugs. They think that's why Mexico has always been poor. They look at the United States and say, "This is a rich and a great country." They forget that it's made up of people from many countries and cultures who emigrated here. The United States has prospered because of its immigrants.

My mother makes the history of Mexico come to life for me. "Mexico is mainly two cultures," she says, "the Indians and the Spanish." The Indians—the Mayas, the Toltecs, the Aztecs—were rich in their cultures. Thousands of years ago they built and decorated temples and pyramids that are there today. They had their own religion with priests and lots of gods and goddesses. People like feather-weavers and goldsmiths who made things with their hands were very important. The Indians knew about the heavens and mathematics when no one else did and they made giant stone calendars.

Then the Spanish beat the Indians and ran Mexico for a long time, maybe hundreds of years. They built Catholic churches. My family is Catholic. I believe in God; sometimes I spend nights talking to Him. When I was young, my mother would say, "If you have a problem, God gives you strength. God will always listen and help." You've heard the saying, God helps those who help themselves? I think of it this way. I ask for help, and God says, "Okay." Well, I have to keep up my end of the bargain. I have to work and God helps along the way.

If you are Mexican, inside you, around you, you feel the Indian and the Spanish cultures. I am both these cultures. On my mom's side, her dad was an Indian, an Aztec. His parents were Aztecs, too. Before my mother was born, her dad fought in the Revolution for a better life and better education for the poor people. Her mom was half Spanish and half Indian. Her mother's mother was from Spain. Her mother's father was also an Indian. Her grandfather went and stole her and they got married.

My dad left home with friends when he was younger than I am and came first to San Diego, then to Los Angeles. He thought the streets would be paved with gold. He doesn't talk much about his past, except he once told me that his father, my grandfather, always said, "Hard work makes a man out of you."

In many ways my dad is American now. He doesn't speak Spanish that well, but he understands everything. And even though my mother doesn't speak English, she understands it. When my father and my mother talk, she speaks to him in Spanish and he answers her in English. I talk to my dad in English and my mother in Spanish. I'm used to it; it's what I've always known. What matters is that I know what I'm about and so do the important people in my life.

I don't understand kids who are angry at their parents and at their culture. You are what you are. You can't do anything about it. If somebody says, "Oh, Mexicans can't do this," I want to prove them wrong. Mexicans have gone through so much hardship. I wish this country realized more what we give back.

My parents say, "You come from a different background, so to get ahead you have to do twice if not three times better than the American-born person. You have to learn the American culture." I listen to them, but then I think about an ideal society where there's a little bit of every culture and it goes together just right. Say there's a part of the United States that's very hot. The problem to solve: What can we do to keep these people from overheating? The people who came here from the tropics have certain secrets of surviving in hot climates. Well, they come along and would say, "When I lived in the tropics, we used to do this, this, and that. We made our buildings with thick walls and a lot of windows. The buildings were white to reflect away the sun." And the others would say, "Hey, what a great idea. It works!" Different ideas would come together and make everything a whole lot better.

If other Mexican immigrants read this, I would tell them, work hard and remember who we are. Don't get into that easy-money stuff. Instead, think of all the good, not all the problems, that lie ahead. We can't climb the whole staircase all at once, just one step at a time. And we should try even harder to help make our ethnic group have a greater voice in the future of America.

Sook

AGE 18, SOUTH KOREAN

I thought, my life is over. I'll die
if I don't go back to my country.

Korea, once called the Hermit Kingdom, is a small Asian nation that suffered centuries of political unrest and economic hardship. By its own historians' account, the peninsula has been invaded nine hundred times. Following World War II, long before Sook was born, the United States and the Soviet Union divided the country in two. The 1950s saw the three-year-long Korean War, which involved North Korea and China fighting against South Korea and a U.S.-commanded multinational United Nations force. Although the economy of South Korea has improved tremendously, two years ago Sook and her family came to America because there were more opportunities here: for her sister who is hearing-impaired, and for Sook, too. This stylesetting junior apologizes for her English and then talks nonstop for the next three hours.

Abandoned! That's how I felt the August we first came to America. I thought, I always believed I could depend on my dad and my mom, but now they are abandoning me. Just like that!

"Because your aunt and uncle have a big house in Washington, you should stay with them and their baby," my dad said. The rest of my family—my parents, a sister, and a brother—would go to Chicago where I had more relatives who said they would help them make some money to get started.

I felt totally left out and totally scared. I stayed inside all day and wrote letters to my friends back home. They had been surprised when I told them I was going to America. They envied me because they didn't like the school we went to. The studying was getting harder and harder. Sometimes you had to stay up the whole night to get ready for tests. Terrible. But they also worried about me. How was I going to get along? I had been studying English in class because starting in junior high everyone has to. It's a requirement to graduate. But I never thought I'd have to really use it. What I learned didn't help me at all. It was just a little grammar and the alphabet, which is nothing like the Korean alphabet.

My friends had a going-away party for me. I didn't cry at the time. But on Thursday, the day we were moving, that was different. The plane was leaving in the morning and they were supposed to be in school. I got to the airport and they were all there. My best girlfriends, my boyfriend, and two other guys.

My mom liked my boyfriend. She and his mom were good friends. Actually, we almost grew up together. But my dad wasn't that happy about him, and especially that morning. Can you imagine, I had to say good-bye to my boyfriend in front of my parents. It was hard. And I knew they were all missing school. This is a big deal over there! Saying good-bye to me was NOT going to be an excuse for the teacher. That moment, I cried a lot. I told them, "I'll be back in two years to visit you. I promise."

My friends wrote me a letter and I read it and read it. They told me they decided that day not to go back to school. They just didn't feel like it. They got drunk instead! And because they cut school, they got in trouble. I thought, ohmigosh, it's all my responsibility. I miss them a lot.

———

Pretty soon, it was September and there was nothing I could do. I had to go to school. Alone. Just before we moved here, my dad had told me, "You have to promise that no matter where you are, you will always be Korean."

"I will, I will," I answered. That day at school, though, he and Mom couldn't help me. I had to do it by myself. I thought, I will be a proud and respectful Korean. But I was in hell! Everyone was giving me strange looks. There were no other Koreans in school. The whole week I saw three other Asians, a Thai girl and two Chinese, but that was it. This was my junior year all over again. I'd just finished it and the American school decided I had to do it again. I thought, my life is over. I'll die if I don't go back to my country!

When I came home, I cried a lot. I told my aunt, "I don't like the school. I want to quit. I will take the GED, the high school equivalency test." My aunt said, "This is what happens to everybody when you move. You'll get over it. Don't cry." When she saw that wasn't helping, she said, "If you don't like it, you could get a job." I thought, okay, I'll do that. I worked for three days at a Kentucky Fried until I got burned from the oil for the french fries. I got so scared, I quit. I swore, "I am never going to work again!"

A month later I moved to Nevada with my second aunt and her husband. I could share a bedroom with my cousin and she could really help me. She's about two years younger than me. We could get along well. I don't know why they didn't think of that first. Going to school there was just fine. I made new friends, mostly Asians. I didn't really have any American friends.

The few I talked to didn't know Korea. I'd tell them, "It's where 'M*A*S*H,' the TV show, happens. The Olympics took place there." If they studied world history, they might be learning about Korea right now because of the Korean War and maybe World War II. But they don't know many details. They don't know that the two powers, America and Russia, wanted to control us; that we didn't have any power and that's why the country is divided. They don't know that in the North, the government is Communist. In the South, where I lived, it isn't. They don't think that my country is as good as here.

My family had lived in Korea for hundreds and hundreds and hundreds of years. And that's not unusual. We lived in the capital of South Korea, Seoul. Seoul has been the capital since the fourteenth century. Today, it is a modern city. There are traffic jams all the time, tall buildings, crowded streets, shopping malls, washing machines, video games, movies, skateboards, Coca-Cola, and pollution.

Most people live in apartments like we did. We were on the fifth floor of a building that was about twenty stories tall. From our window, we could see other apartment buildings, a big street, and a parking lot.

Six of us lived in the four rooms: my parents, my sister, my brother, and my grandmother. Most of the old people, they believe in Buddha. My grandmother is Buddhist. The younger people are Catholic or Christian. We are Christian, but I don't go that much. My father was a college graduate and worked for the car company Hyundai. For a few years my mother ran a small store, but most of the time she only worked at home.

In Korea in junior and senior high, you have to wear uniforms and have your hair in the style that the school wants. If it gets too long, you get in trouble and you have to go to the dean's office. And you can't get perms! Nail polish? No way! The parents' attitude is you have to respect the teachers. You can't be rude to them. You go to school with that in mind.

The public school I went to had real big classes, fifty or sixty kids in each room. You know how here in the United States you come to school to play, for fun, especially in senior high, and then in college you study a lot? In Korea, it's the opposite. Once you get to junior high, it's really strict; and it keeps getting stricter. You have to study, study, study. You do everything you can just to get into college. And then, if you make it, if you get to college, you can relax and goof off. Classes are not really hard and no one really studies. They just have fun because most students have been studying so hard they never had fun before. If you go to college in Korea, your future is pretty secure.

I like English. It sounds soft and romantic.

After I was here for a year, my dad and mom called and said they were settled. I could live with them again, now in Chicago. I was happy, but still, all over again, I had to go to a new school. I had to meet new friends. And all over again, I had to be a junior! The first day of school I was walking down the hallway, when I heard someone say "Hi" in Korean. I turned around and then I realized that there were other Koreans and other Asians in this school. At first I was so excited, I said "Hi," but then almost right away it got weird.

They could tell by my last name that I was Korean. But at this school they think they have to keep company with just themselves. They don't want to mingle with people from anywhere but Korea. They don't want to join other people. And that's part of the problem. They could be a big help for people who just moved here. They were supposed to help me. When a new Korean person comes, the newer ones help the newest ones. It keeps going on and on.

But I found out it's not always like that. These kids formed a clique. They immediately started saying things like, "Where does she come from?" "I don't think she just moved here." "I don't like the way she dresses, the way she talks, the way she acts." "I can't stand her." Some of them saw me say "Hi" to a black girl. They said, "Why did you say 'Hi' to her? She's black!" I said, "My life is living here. I need to open my mind to all people."

Once in my English class, where I sit, someone had left me this long letter. It was in Korean and filled with curses. I couldn't believe it. It said, "Who do you think you are? Someone special? Don't be snotty." All the time they would talk about me behind my back. They'd look for me in the hallway. They'd give me dirty looks. I made friends with a Chinese girl and four Korean girls told her to stay away from me. I hated it.

I decided I don't need their help. I want to live here and I want to speak this language. I like English. It sounds soft and romantic. Anyway, some of them who moved here five or six years ago still really can't speak English. I was shocked. I thought, they never use English. They only hear and use it with their teachers. Even when they watch TV, they watch Korean cable! If I just try to look for all the people who came from my same country, and I stay with them the way I did in my country, there will be no difference between being there and living here.

For me, and maybe for all immigrants, what's best I decided is that once you move here, you have to be like one of these American people. Try to hang around with people who speak English. It doesn't have to be just American people, but with people who speak good English and who act like Americans. That wasn't the reason, though, that I noticed my new boyfriend.

He's an American-born Chinese, second generation. He knows how to say "Hello" in Chinese and that's about it. He's in my math class and I liked him right away. I didn't say anything, because it was embarrassing. In Korea, much much more than here, the man is the boss. It's always more important to have a boy child than a girl. The opportunities go to men first. And they are supposed to ask you out first. So we just talked, and then finally around Christmas, he asked me out. I was acting like—excited! It's been six months now.

My mom knows and my dad does, too, but he doesn't take it too seriously. He just makes a lot of faces. We are only allowed to go out once a week on Fridays, and I have to be home at ten or eleven. We go out to a movie, get pizza, or go bowling. But then maybe twice the whole year if there's a party, I can stay out a little later. The important thing is that they know where I am. Then, they don't really mind. I'm the oldest one and the oldest one has to be perfect to show the younger ones.

I try to be a good example. I have a part-time job as a cashier in a little grocery store where I work ten hours each day on Saturdays and Sundays. We got the class transcript and I was ranked fifteenth out of more than four hundred students. I got a pass from the dean and I called my dad. He was so happy, too.

He said, "What do you want?"

"I want a car."

"Bye," and he hung up the phone laughing. But I knew he was proud.

And I'm proud of my dad, too. One of the reasons we came to America was he wanted to own a business. At first he didn't know what kind of business to start. He worked in a fruit and vegetable store. To see if he wanted to own one, he had to know how things worked. But it was too hard work. He said. "No way! I'd ruin my back in that business, carrying and loading all the boxes of vegetables!"

So my dad started working in a dry cleaning store. He didn't get paid; he just volunteered. Then later he found out it was for sale. He told the owner, "I'll buy this store." And he did.

He could do that because he got money from a "keh." A keh is sort of like a club. A group of Koreans get together and each month they put the same amount of money together. Then right away one of the people gets all of the money. One month, it was my father's time to take it.

My mom worries a little about him being robbed. She doesn't like him to be alone most of the time. But at first when he opened up, there was only one employee. He came after one o'clock in the day. And now he's hired another guy. He opens with my dad and stays until nine. My father's day is nine to nine and Saturday it's until 10:00 P.M. Plus the time getting there and back. It takes forty minutes to get there. But the store is doing okay.

I like being with my parents. The most bad that ever happens is sometimes my dad and I have little fights. Like my dad doesn't like the color of my nail polish.

He says, "That's too dark."

And I go, "It's fine."

"Well, that's what you think, but I think it's too dark."

"It's my nails."

I know they only want what is best for me. Like my mom worries about gangs. I do, too. That really bothers me. They even kill each other. About three weeks ago, a Chinese guy got shot near my home. He was in my school. Once he asked me out, but I didn't like the way he did his hair, all spiked up. He looked scary. Ever since then, he'd say "Hi" to me and I said "Hi" back. Later, I didn't see him for a long time. I heard he'd dropped out of school. Well, he's the one who got shot and it was in all the newspapers. My dad told me he read it in the Korean newspaper, too. Some thought the ones who shot him were Korean.

There are Korean gangs, too. I think only a few older high school kids are in them. More are those in their twenties, more Koreans who were born here. When you just move here, you're not brave enough to join with them.

I've been in America two years and I'm finally going to be a senior. I like being here definitely. I want to go to college and major in pharmacy. I use as my hero for this, my second uncle. He's great. When my aunt was marrying him in my country, he was nothing. Everybody told her she shouldn't marry him, but she did. Oh, the way we treated him! We didn't respect him at all.

They came here to America and he didn't know how to speak a word of English. Now they've been here six years and he's a pharmacist. He makes a lot of money, they have a nice house, and when I went to where he works, he introduced me to his staff. I was shocked. They all understood his English! I said, "This is a miracle!" And he answered, "Sook, America is where miracles come true."

Anna

AGE 17, GREEK

There is no adolescence in Greece.
You go from
boy to man . . . girl to woman.

Greece is a rocky peninsula dipping into the Mediterranean Sea surrounded by islands. The history of Europe and western civilization began with Greece, and it is the bridge between that world and Asia. It gave us a range of gifts, from democracy to the Olympics. The spring that Anna turned eleven, she and her family left their home, a placid Greek island village, population five hundred, and emigrated to the United States. Now, six years later, she is an outgoing and opinionated senior. We catch up with her after her job at the school store. Anna begins by talking about her parents.

———

I'm becoming an American and my parents are afraid of that. I try to reassure them. I tell them, "Look, it's me. You may not always know me, but I'm still me."

When I was a little kid, I thought my parents were high and mighty, smart and strong. But now, even though I love them both, at times I see them as two children.

Take how they deal with things, how they solve their problems. Learning to be an American is very complex. And sometimes, many times, when we have a crisis, my parents don't really know how to handle it. They don't know that I am learning. The result? I often feel I'm here by myself. In the beginning, I went through a lot of things at school. The other students used to hurt me a lot. My parents didn't know how to come to me and say, "Let's talk about it. Don't worry. We understand it is hard to adjust to a new culture." They didn't know what to do, because their parents didn't have to do it for them.

Then, when I did begin to learn all these new, exciting things, I wanted to share them. I'm the youngest in my family with an older brother and sister. Neither of them went to school here; only I did. Well, my brother, forget it. He only cared about himself. Like if I said something to him about earth science, because that's my favorite subject, he changed the topic and told me about his work, mechanics. He tried to compete with me to show that he knew more than I did. My sister was all involved in her work, and then her husband, so I couldn't bother her. The only people left were my parents.

Once I understood English, once I started to see a whole American world out there that I never knew existed, a world that you don't see in Greece, I felt a little distant from them. The distance grew. They would be proud of me, but they also began to feel threatened. My new knowledge had no meaning for them. This has been hard and sad for all of us.

My parents' philosophy is that, "We support you and you have to take care of us when we're old." They push me; they push my brother and sister. "You can't leave your parents out there in the world especially when we don't know English. We are your responsibility." I think that is their fear speaking and their fear that I am changing.

When we arrived in America, my brother was eighteen. At that age, he was already a man. At fifteen he had become a mechanic. There is no adolescence in Greece. You go from boy to man. It's the culture. A lot of kids don't even go to junior high school. If you're smart and you go, when you get out at fifteen or sixteen, you start work. That's when you're a man.

It's the same thing for girls. That's one place where they don't discriminate. You go from being a girl directly to the responsibilities of being a woman, and that means getting married. If you're not attractive to the opposite sex, you better become smart. Some of my best friends from my island (let's call it Thiros) are already married and one has a child. The Greek husband is supposed to be older than the wife. Women are considered ready for marriage at sixteen. The men are ready at about twenty-one, twenty-two; I guess that's because they first have to go into the army.

Of course, having a family is important, too, and sticking together in a family. Half the town where I lived are relatives, cousins, aunts, everything. My great-grandmother had around twelve children. They all got married, but at the farthest, they are only an hour away. They still come back to see her.

Up until the tourists started coming to Thiros, I

think it was a pretty similar culture and life-style for centuries. Most marriages take place between people who live on the same island. You go on the outside, you have to pay for the boat and everything. It's too hard.

It was nice to be raised there, comfortable and fun. Thiros was mountainous, except on the edges at the water. That's where most of the people lived. The best thing about the island was taking trips in the spring when all the flowers were in bloom. Horizontally east to west, it would take one hour to drive across Thiros; vertically from south to north, about four hours.

People earn their living mostly by farming and fishing. My father used to grow things. My mother worked at home and sometimes worked with him in the small bit of land we had. My father also owned an old truck. He used it to carry supplies and farming stuff, vegetables and produce, to the market from the farms. People there aren't really competitive the way they are here in America. They don't say, "Help me take my fruit to the market, but don't help my neighbor." They realize to survive you have to do it together.

In Greece, mythology came first, before religion. When Greek Orthodox, that's a Christian religion, came in, the Greeks adapted it to fit some of the myths. And geography is mixed in with mythology, too. I love myths with all the gods and goddesses. The stories are taught in school starting in third grade. One of my favorite gods is Poseidon, the god of water and of the islands. If you live on an island that is devoted mostly to fishing, Poseidon tends to be popular. Hercules used to be my favorite story before I found out he is stupid. He's the one who is the strongest man on earth and the son of the main god, Zeus. There's Athena, the goddess of brains, although her namesakes don't always have them. And Icarus who went too close to the sun and melted the feathers off his back. One of the islands is named after him.

Fighting with the Turks is another part of life in Greece. At some time in our history, hundreds of years ago, Turkey ruled Greece. Then in a war in the 1800s, we won our independence and regained our land. There's a whole story and we celebrate it.

Through the Second World War, again, we were fighting with the Turkish. They have a different religion, mostly Muslim, and religion is strong. Maybe that's why Greeks and Turks don't like each other. The old people keep telling us stories about the Turks being terrible to us. We get an idea when we're children that they are evil barbarians. I don't see them that way, but that's what we are taught.

On my island they have this story about a woman whose mother was Christian and her Turkish father was Muslim. One day her father found out that she was Christian, too. She ran from him, but he caught her and cut off her head. They tell us this story, and then, we tell the next generation.

All day long, six days a week, my father washed dishes, my mother and my sister sewed.

One summer my aunt, who already lived in America, came to Greece for a visit. She jokingly said, "Why don't you come live there, too." My father always looked for a better job and a better way of life. So he said to my mother, "Why not try it." It took about two years to get all the paperwork, the visa and passports and tests before we could go. I heard my parents talking about it and I asked my mother. She said, "Yes, we're going to America." In Greece we don't have a way to "break it to the children." We just tell them. Kids don't have any choice in the matter.

Parting was hard, but I like to go on new adventures. I have a picture of me from the day we left. I had on a yellow dress and new black shoes. I was this cute, skinny little girl. We flew to Boston and my aunt met us at the airport. At the end of a big corridor, there she was. We hadn't seen her for a long time, and at first we didn't recognize her. It was a little tense. I didn't speak any American, and my cousins who were born here didn't speak much Greek.

On the ride to my relatives' house, I thought, "Wow! This place is huge!" I couldn't believe the numbers of roads and cars and intersections and buildings. On my island the village is on a hill. They have only one main street and that is windy.

After we arrived, my parents seemed to have a plan. Because we couldn't live with my aunt forever, we found a house to rent. Living there in the beginning was kind of like camping out. We didn't have beds, so we slept on the floor. Then we got some furniture from these other Greek people who were leaving. There is a Greek community and they try to help each other. They feel for us. They remember.

The jobs were next. With the Greek connections, my father found a job washing dishes in a restaurant. My mother knew how to sew. She and my sister went to work in a factory where everybody is sitting one next to the other at sewing machines. All day long, six days a week, my father washed dishes, my mother and my sister sewed. I was told not to go outside in the yard for fear of whatever. Instead I stayed home, watching TV to learn some English.

When I finally enrolled in school, because I didn't have a report card from Thiros showing that I passed fifth grade, they put me back a year to the fourth grade. I had worked for a lot of years and I didn't think it was fair. But what could I do? I started making friends, and because they were immigrants, too, English was the language we all used. My best friend was from Cambodia. The neighbors picked on her family and called them Cambos. She never talked about how she escaped from her country, but her face had this look that said, "I've been through a terrible time."

———

Things are falling into place for my family, now. With my brother, I guess he felt it was time to get married. At twenty-two he went back to Thiros, met a girl, and married her. Big event, ta-dah! Before that, he'd never even dated. His social life had been to go out with the guys. His wife was sixteen when they married, and uneducated. My sister married a guy from Greece and is still a seamstress.

My father is a chef and the boss asks his advice. My mother's moved up, too. She makes beautiful wedding dresses for $5.99 an hour. My whole life plan is that I'll go to college. I will become an accountant. I will work, save a lot of money, and then go back to school to take psychology, just to learn about it, to enjoy it. I've always been interested in why people act the way they do. I began reading about psychology, dreams, hypnosis. I'd think, why do you fall in love with a certain person and not another? Why do I like stories about vampires? Why do some people leave my island, Thiros, to come to America and others don't?

Thiros is not a place to live. It's a place to go visit, to live in your old life. Think of it as Florida! It's very peaceful, but there's not much happening. In America you have all these things. You have jobs, first of all. If you are willing to work very hard, there's always a place in the Greek community where they could make a job for you. Here, the way I see it, you have life. In Thiros, you just have a small part of it, the dream.

Martha

AGE 16, DOMINICAN

My mother tells me that my
father loved to dance the merengue
more than he loved us.

The Dominican Republic shares the island of Hispaniola with the country of Haiti. A ridge of soaring mountains divides them. Located in the Caribbean, this Spanish-speaking nation is the size of Maryland and Massachusetts combined, but with half their population, six and a half million. Santo Domingo, the capital, founded in 1496, is the oldest European settlement in the Western Hemisphere. "Today," says Martha, "there are more Dominicans in New York City than in the town where I was born." One steamy June afternoon, we talk in the offices of a Bronx, New York, job placement center for high school students. With Martha is Brenda, her cousin, best friend, and occasional translator. Martha, who emigrated five years ago, begins with a brief history of her country and her family.

The Dominican Republic is a little country that everybody's taken advantage of. Columbus landed there in 1492 and that started it all. The Spanish, the French, the Americans, and then the people from Haiti were in there at some time, too, taking advantage of my people. February 27 is Dominican Independence Day, the day we liberated ourselves from the Haitians.

My great-grandmothers on both sides were from Spain. They were white. My grandfather on my mother's side was from the Indians, the Arawak. He had the brown skin and very fine hair. His wife, my mother's mother, practiced the religion "Brujería," spiritism. She became an important witch. She was dead three years before I was born, but they say she was very good. In the Dominican Republic it's against the law to practice spiritism. The government just allows what they call the "real religions" like Catholic and Pentecostal.

Some people still practice witchcraft, but not openly. It's like voodoo and Santería, except voodoo is more from Haiti and Santería, with the animal sacrifices, is more from Cuba, Afro-Cuban. With spiritism, we don't have animal sacrifices. We sit down and the medium calls different spirits. Some people put fruit out for them, but more often it's tobacco or rum. The spirits like to party. They like alcohol. I was surprised when I came to the United States and saw people advertising themselves as practicing spiritism.

I don't know that much about the rest of my relatives. I guess we have a couple of negroes in there, too, maybe on my mother's side, because our hair is not so fine anymore. I don't know what moment they got into the family, though. Anyway, I'm a mixture of black and white. The majority of people in my country are like that. We call them mulattoes.

We also have a lot of prejudice there. I'm going to tell you this. Once I went to a restaurant in the Dominican and this lady said if they served me, that "negra"— that's like saying that "nigger"—that she was leaving the restaurant. The people from there might tell you that we're not prejudiced, but that's a joke. And it's based on the color of our skin—the whiter the better. I have never felt the prejudice in the United States that I felt in my country. Sometimes people made me feel like s———.

Now don't get me wrong. The Dominican is a beautiful country, a great resort, and you can find anything you want, if you have money. You will find people from the jet set there, people enjoying vacations. If you have money, you will live like a king, even more than here. And the people who have money are the most prejudiced. They treat the poor people like garbage! They have made it part of the culture that when we introduce someone, we must use your title. If we leave out the title, we are insulting you. The military is very important, also. If someone says, "My father is a captain," we know you are threatening us. If we don't have a title, we are nobody.

We grow up hearing and talking about "Nueva Yorque"— New York. That is where everybody is rich and wears gold chains.

My mother tells me that for many years in the Dominican, you are either rich-rich or you are poor. The people live under the rule of dictators. Now there is a democratic government. Life improves a little, but still the United States gives my country a lot of money. We grow up hearing and talking about "Nueva Yorque"—New York. That is where everybody is rich and wears gold chains.

Unemployment is really high in my country and those few who have money don't want to invest it there because the country hasn't been stabilized for the longest time. So poor people come to America for better jobs and rich people come here to make more money. At least, this is what my mother says.

Not so long after I was born, my father left. My mother tells me that he loved to dance the merengue more than he loved us. The merengue is LIFE in my country, but my mother says it shouldn't be more important than your family. He shouldn't have run out on her when she had no money and a little baby. I don't see him and his family very much.

The only thing she could think of to do was to move to New York. She came here illegal, and that's all I know. I was only a year old. She got a job taking care of other people's babies. I lived with my aunt, my uncle, and my five cousins. They took care of me.

Every Christmas my mother would come visit. I thought of her as a stranger. She called me sometimes but I didn't always want to talk to her. I didn't feel very warm toward her. I felt better toward my aunt. Then when I was ten my aunt told me that I was going to New York. She said it had been very hard for my mother to get papers for me, but after two years of trying, she did.

The next thing I knew I was on a bus to Santo

Domingo and then to an airplane where I could drink all the Coca-Cola I wanted. I cried the minute the plane landed at JFK [Airport] and I was still crying when we got to my mother's apartment in the Bronx. I cried for fourteen straight days. Then my mother said, "I'm tired of your crying. Settle down or I'm going to send you back." That was the start of her "talks" with me.

I have talks and rules for everything. My mother's favorite is this: "Be careful when you go out. Open your eyes and close your legs. Study to get good grades. Have a career." And I have a curfew. If I break it, I'm in forever. My mother says, "I give you a curfew of nine and you want nine-thirty. I say ten and you want ten-thirty. The more I tell you something, the more you want."

I'm allowed a total of fifteen minutes, three calls, on the phone each day. Brenda calls me, five minutes. I time it. For six months I couldn't use the phone at all because a bill had come in for $150. My mother put a lock on it, kept the only key, and said, "You should be grateful for a phone."

I couldn't wear makeup until last year, when I turned fifteen. I couldn't date until after my sixteenth birthday, two months ago. I brought a guy home that I liked and my mother put him by the open window in the kitchen and asked him questions. "What do you hope to pursue?" "What are your intentions with my daughter?" She told me, "If I don't like his answers, there's a bat behind the curtain that's going to come out!" It made the guy nervous.

Then he had to ask my mother permission to ask me out. She said, "Okay," but we still had to have a chaperone—her. A good Dominican girl is never supposed to be alone with a guy. We couldn't go out on a real date. He could only come over and sit on the couch and watch TV with us. So what I did was told my mother I was going to the library, but instead I met him.

Another thing is that she won't let me be on the volleyball team. She says, "Volleyball isn't going to get you anywhere. It's better in school, not on the street." But I'm really good at it, one of the best. After school Brenda and I play handball at some courts near here. We're usually the only girls playing. Once the guys wanted to play with us and we beat them! They said, "It's embarrassing. Don't tell anyone that two girls beat us."

I suppose that someday I will become a U.S. citizen. My mother is. A couple years ago she paid $250 to some lawyer to start the paperwork, and now he tells her no one can find my records. I'm a lost person. My mother laughed when she told me that. I said, "I'm ready to be on my own now, get my own apartment. I feel American now." She laughed some more.

Von

AGE 20, VIETNAMESE

*They know the boat people often
have money and gold. They steal
the females and rape them and force
them into prostitution in Thailand.
They are pirates.*

Vietnam, bordered on the north by China and on the
west by Laos and Cambodia [Kampuchea], has a coast-
line of beaches washed by the South China Sea. The
recorded history of this S-shaped nation begins before
the birth of Christ, and includes centuries of domina-
tion by China, colonization by France, and occupation
by Japan. When most Americans think of Vietnam, we
think of what we call the "Vietnam War." Our involve-
ment began in 1955, shortly after the country was
divided into North Vietnam and South Vietnam; we
backed the authoritarian South Vietnam president,
Ngo Dinh Diem. By the mid-1960s we were partici-
pants in a full-scale war between the Communist
northern forces, the Viet Cong, and the southern forces

aided by U.S. troops. On April 30, 1975, Saigon, the capital of South Vietnam, fell, ending this stage of the tragedy that by then had cost 1.3 million Vietnamese and 56,000 American lives. Von is a survivor of that war and the devastating years that followed. Today when you see him—slim, handsome, with an optimistic and ready grin—it's hard to imagine what his eyes have seen. Over a series of days, we met in hours sandwiched between his busy schedule of school and work. He begins at his beginning.

———

I was born in Saigon. My father was a navy officer for South Vietnam. He worked for the United States government. I have three brothers and three sisters. I am number four. I'm the only one who came to America with my father. My mother and the rest of them are still in Vietnam. Sometimes on Sundays after church, my father and I talk about our past memories, what brought us here and of the future. I decided that someday I would like to write of my family, and of him and me together. You are the first person I ever told my family's story.

———

They called those months in 1972 the Hot Summer because of all the bombing and the many deaths. Those are my first memories. I was four years old, and my father had moved from Saigon to Da Nang, in the central part of the country. We went along with him. From Laos on the west side of Vietnam, the Communists, the Viet Cong, would sneak into Vietnam and fight and fight against the marines.

On the other side of Da Nang is the sea. My father

was fighting on that side. He worked on a PT boat. Every night he had to go out to the sea. Sometimes his boat would be blown up and he'd get thrown in the water. He had almost died many times.

There was so much fighting. We got attacked from the land and the mountains and the sea. Every night, every month, bombs dropping from the South Vietnam army attacking the North Vietnam army. Every night for years and years, we and our neighbors had to run to hide in the bomb-shelter underground. We would cook and eat there. We waited for the bombing to be over. Then we would go back home until it happened again. It was hard to sleep.

My mother tried to help us. She is Buddhist, but my father is Catholic. When she got married to him, she joined with him. We always believe in the Virgin Mary. In the bomb shelter we would pray. The Virgin Mary is a miracle. When I get afraid, I always pray and she helps me.

We had a better life than most families because my father was an officer. We had people who took us to school and took us back home. It was a private Catholic school. I don't remember much about it. Bombs fell during the day, too, always interrupting the teaching.

Finally my mother said, "This is not good for a life." She wanted to return to Saigon. We still had a home there. My mother's mother, my grandmother, was living there. She would write us and say, "Here the kids go to school. It is nice." We discussed it with my mother. "Why should we stay in Da Nang? Grandma has everything. Here we run up and down, up and down with the interruptions for the bombs. And Daddy is never home with us."

In Saigon, my father's friends said, "You want to

come back? You got a good job right here." My father had an idea that Saigon might fall, that the Communists would take it. At the last moment, a group of generals met together and they said, "We might be able to keep the Communists in the middle of the country. From there to the north will belong to them. The south will be the South Vietnamese government."

My father said, "Okay, we leave."

———

When we left Da Nang in 1975, we started with our possessions, but we'd go so far and then we had to leave some and we'd go farther and we'd leave some more. When we got halfway to Saigon, the Communists took Da Nang. So many people were trying to get into Saigon. The Communists hadn't taken the South yet, but they were still attacking.

People were being killed by the Communists. Many families lost their kids and their mothers and fathers. We were lucky. Because my father was in a high position, we had a letter giving us permission to get on board a ship which took us to safety on an island.

When we got there, my father said, "Let's wait and see what happens with the war before we take the next boat to Saigon." But all the families had to live in a shelter, a "para." It was a building that had been used as prison. The South Vietnamese government kept Communists there. They had put bombs and grenades and boobytraps hidden underground around the building to keep the prisoners from escaping. My mother said, "This not safe. All there is is a warning sign. I don't like it."

My father agreed. He didn't know until much later that if we had stayed on that one island, they took all the people to Thailand and then on to the United States. Today we would all be here together.

———

When we got to Saigon, my father got the job he had been told about, assistant commander of a navy base. But after one week, on the night of April 30, 1975, the Communists came into Saigon and attacked the base. It was so crazy and so scary. We couldn't go to him and he couldn't leave his base, get us, and take us back with him.

He knew everything was lost.

My father had to go on a ship to Thailand with all the military from the navy base. When he got there he said, "I left my family behind. The Communists might come and kill them." The Americans in Thailand said, "You must go to the United States. You cannot return to Saigon. You will get killed." My father said, "I must return for my family."

He changed out of his military clothes and he sneaked under a boiler tank on a ship. The Americans came looking for him. They checked around, but when they didn't see anything, they left. My father stayed hidden and the ship pulled out. He headed back to Vietnam knowing that it had fallen. He said, "If my family dies, I want us to die together, not apart."

When the ship got closer to Vietnam, my father saw some fishermen. He jumped ship and went with them the rest of the way back. We had no news from my father. We wanted to go to the base to look for him, but anyone who went near the base had been killed. The Communists shot them all.

So the Communists wouldn't find anything, we gathered together my father's photographs and his uniforms and medals. He had many medals. We kept one or two small things and hid them very carefully. The rest we burned. We burned my father's memories. Even today, he remembers, and he's always sad. All he worked so hard for.

A long time ago before I was born, my father had studied with the military in the United States for six months. He went to Hollywood and loved it! He brought a picture book back from California. Once, after the Communists took over, I took the book from its hiding place. I didn't read English, of course, but I looked at the pictures and I liked them so much! I said, "WOW, this is America! In my mind I said, "How can I get here?" I didn't know where it was, but I knew they had cars and houses and kids and so happy and food! I said, "Maybe someday I be there."

We had locked all the doors and the Communists came and banged. They said, "Where is your father?"

"We don't know."

They said, "You must tell us!"

Three weeks later my father sneaked back into Saigon in his civilian clothes. We were together again!

———

The Communists, the way they look for you, they don't say, "We're going to take you to jail." They say, "We just want to see you." So they went to my house and they said to my father, "All former officers in the South Vietnam army must go to study. You have to go to be re-educated." My father thought, oh, Communists give people another chance. We don't go to jail; we go to school!

They told my father, "We educate you for only three months and then you will come back to your family." My father was so happy. He thought, the new government is not like the Soviet government. This one is going to treat everybody equal. My brother made a suitcase for my father. He put a few things in it and took him to a car where the government met him and took him away. My father had only been with us for two weeks.

———

Three months went by and no news.

Another week went by. Another month. Another year. No news at all. We asked and the Communist government said, "They are fine. They're in school."

My mother said, "Can you help? Where are they, so we can visit."

"Okay," they said, "we'll let you know."

———

We really suffered. All the money my father had saved during the war, the government took. Over the years, though, he had also given money to my grandmother and she bought some gold to keep for our security. She gave it to us and told my mother, "You have to do something. Try to open a business so you can keep the money alive. You have a lot of kids." My mother knew she was right. We didn't know if my father would ever come back to take care of the family again.

My father was about forty-five years old. My mother was around forty. She didn't know anything about business. She came from an educated and wealthy family. But by that time, because food had gotten very expensive, my mother decided she would get into the rice business. We bought a kilo of rice on the black market for maybe five dollars, and we took it to the local market to sell for five dollars and fifty cents. That's how it worked. But we had only a little money and we could only buy a little. We didn't make a profit.

After the second year, my mother ran out of all the money. She had to start selling the few things we had left in the house. There was her favorite vase that had been her grandmother's. And we had a Honda motorcycle to help us in our business. That was all. We sold them to eat.

My oldest brother left the house to find work. When he filled out applications for jobs, he said his father was dead. He told my mother, though, "I won't get married until we are all safe together again."

We applied to school, but they said, "No, your family is not acceptable. Your father was in the military. If you want to get back into school, you have to wait until your father returns." My mother tried to educate us at home. We would read the newspaper. We would find books and read, read, read. My grandmother said, "Think positive." For six years, I had no school.

———

After two and a half years, somebody brought us a letter from my father. "He's still alive!" we said. He sent his wedding ring in the letter. He told my mother, "If you run out of money, sell the ring to take care of the kids. I might be home and I might not."

My mother said, "Oh, my God."

Then another day the government sent us a letter. They gave my mother permission to go to see him. They said she could visit because he was so good. He worked very hard in the camp. He didn't make trouble, so they gave him a break. They told him, "We will allow your wife to see you one time for two hours."

My father had asked in the letter, "If they let us meet, would you be kind enough to bring me some cigarettes and something sweet. I'd like to smoke and eat something sweet with my tea." My mother found some sugar and baked a cake and she bought him some cigarettes.

She traveled a week to get there. She had to take a boat to an island and then the government took her to the jungle part where the concentration camp was. Few people were allowed to go to that concentration camp. Even the people on the island didn't know much.

When my mother got there, oh, she couldn't believe it! My father was so skinny! So old! His hair all turned white. My father and my mother were so sad. This was a concentration camp for all the educated people. Pharmacists. Doctors. Political people. Lawyers. Scientists. Military. The people watching them were not educated. They were young boys, sixteen, seventeen years old, and they treated the prisoners like animals. My father said, "Some of us commit suicide. We cannot take it anymore. Others get killed. The guards make up stories to try to make us crazy. Whoever can think positive is still alive. If we think negative, we are dead."

He had to work from six o'clock in the morning to nine o'clock in the evening. He had to chop the wood and take care of the shrimp that the government would then export to other countries. They would give them so little food for an entire day, and never shrimp. My father worked 365 days a year. No breaks. No vacations. For three years. Once a year, only on New Year's Day, the Communist guards said, "You will have a break today on your mental training, but not your physical. You still have to work but we cancel the daily lecture."

They lectured them about the bad former government and good things about the new government. They always said, "You have to tell the truth. What were you doing in the war? What kind of an officer were you?" My father always said, "I was a chef." If he had said something that was bad to the Communist people, they would send him to the north to torture and death.

One day this boy, this guard, said, "You're an old man. You say you were a chef, but I know you weren't." My father happened to look in his eyes, and the boy slapped and hit him for an hour in front of all the people. Just because my father had looked at him. If he talked back, he would never return. My father tells me these stories now that we are in America. He tells me, "At night they take and shoot some men."

Suddenly, six months after my mother had seen my father, he got released from the concentration camp. We were so happy! When he walked in the door, it was a big change in how he looked, but he said, "I'm OUT! I'm not sad anymore!"

He was only back home a few days before the government said, "You are not allowed to stay in the city. You must go stay in the countryside. You can't be with your wife, but you can take one kid if you want." Again, he had to leave my mother. This time, though, he took me with him. We were sent to a place not only for the military, but for the poor people. It was right next to the border between Cambodia and Vietnam.

The government gave us a little land and food and a house made out of bamboo and coconut leaves. I helped my father grow rice and fruit and corn and potatoes. This was about 1978. For the first six months at the border, there was no fighting. Then the Vietnamese government started fighting with the Cambodians. The Cambodian leader Pol Pot and his people were so mean and awful! They would come with a knife and chop off the heads of many of the people who lived around us. More and more people were getting killed. At night the Cambodians would burn down our neighbors' homes. They'd run outside and say, "Oh, please help us. Don't kill us." And they'd be killed.

The Vietnamese started shooting the cannons and the bombs over to Cambodia, to Kampuchea. Each night it looked like lightning in the sky, like it had been when I was in Da Nang, like it had been in Saigon. We were caught in the middle again with the Vietnam government army pushing on one side and Pol Pot's people pushing on the other. The people, us, we got killed.

One day they told my father, "You, tomorrow, because you were an officer, you must go and clean out the grenades." The Cambodians put grenades under the trees. They put boobytraps everywhere. In the morning when we went to the farms and started working, sometimes people blew up. They blew off their legs and their arms and often they get killed.

Of course my father didn't say "no" to them. He said, "When?" To me he said, "Oh, my God. I have to risk my life for this? NO! I can't take anymore." My father, he could not sleep. He thought, it's my life. All this time I work to become a good man. I come back and for this? I will die for nothing? Should I leave or should I stay? If I stay, I will get killed. He kept what he planned a secret. He just said to me, "You and me, we're leaving. We must go back to your mother."

At six o'clock in the morning, we were supposed to be in the mission at work. But at two o'clock at night, we left the house. They weren't strict with him anymore. They let him be free, because they knew him. They knew he'd been in a concentration camp. And they knew he was very good. They didn't think he would leave. It was dark out and I was afraid. Even in the countryside, they have security guards. We did not go on the road. We sneaked through the trees. Finally we got to a place where we could take a bus. We had little money left for the month, but I was so young, my father didn't have to pay for my bus ticket.

We got back to Saigon, but we could just see my mother for a few hours. It was too dangerous for everybody if we stayed. Too soon, he had to say to my mother, "I must leave you." To me he said, "I must take a younger son with me, you. I take you because you suffer so much. You have a feeling."

I always cared for my mother. I always helped her. My mother said to my father, "Von will be good." She was crying so much. She said, "This is right. This is the way we have to do it. You must leave me."

She said to me, "You take care of your father." And she told my father, "Take care of Von. Get him schooling." My brothers and sisters just looked at me. They were so sad. They knew we were leaving, even though my father didn't tell them. If he told them, they would say, "Why do you take Von? You don't love me?"

My mother said, "I love you." And we left.

———

At that time, many South Vietnamese people were trying to sneak out of the country. They were looking for navy men who knew how to row the boat, who knew how to get to Thailand. Do you know anything about the boat people? They make a boat and they sail and they try to get to freedom. My father was on the sea for almost twenty-five years. Some people learned this and they said to him, "We offer you a job. We make a fake ID for you and your son. We take care of a boat. We get food and you two can go with us."

My father said, "Okay." But somehow the Communists found out and took the boat and the money, too. He was afraid the government might be looking for him. "I must leave you," he told the people.

My father found another connection. This time poor, poor people came to him. They could pay him no money, but they had a boat. For three months, my father prepared. He mended the motor. He bought a map, a compass. Then with the boat, my father and I sneaked out to the river. We were picking up people as we were going along. People here, people there, all poor, country people who wanted to escape to a better life.

There were fifty-two people in a twelve-foot-long boat. We could not move. I sat with my knees in my face. I could not lie down. There were a lot of men, and a few women. There were some kids, but most of the people were in their early twenties. I was maybe eleven or twelve.

We left on a rainy night. There were military police boats out in the sea looking for the escape boats, looking for the boat people. But with the rain, they went inside. We go and go and go. One night and the next day in the evening, we went all the way down the river to the sea because my father rowed so fast. We go and go and go. We were going to Indonesia. My father knew we shouldn't go to Thailand, because there were a lot of pirates. Most of the people who went to Thailand got killed. After four days we saw a blinking light! Oh, we thought, that's an American ship! We first saw the light around two in the morning and by six we could see the boat.

The boat was all black. It was so big and it said "Thailand" on it. My father told me, "They are dangerous people." We were afraid they would attack us. They know the boat people often have money and gold. They steal the females and rape them and force them into prostitution in Thailand. They are pirates.

My father went into the kitchen and took charcoal. He put it on the women's faces. He wanted to help camouflage them in the dark. We only had one gun, a shotgun. The people were saying, "What should we do? Shoot them?"

My father said, "No, we cannot. There are so many of them. If we shoot at them, they will definitely kill us. It is better to let them rob us."

They came on board our little boat. They had knives and hammers. My father said, "Try to act cool." I was so scared, I was shaking. Even my feet were shaking. They ordered all the men to go onto their big ship. I was so small that one man took my hand, picked me up, and threw me to another man on their ship. It looked so far and the ship was rocking that I was afraid they would miss me and I would fall into the sea. They would not bother to save me.

The pirates went around our boat checking for gold. They asked for watches and rings and money and said, "If you lie, we'll throw you into the sea." Everybody gave them everything they had, all their savings for their new lives. But after that the pirates gave us food. We were all very hungry people. They took us back to our boat. We were lucky. They didn't kill us. I guess they felt sorry for us.

We were back alone on the sea and then we saw some more big, big ships. One was from Holland, another from Italy. They saw us and didn't stop! We lay there. We were so hot. Every time we saw a big ship we got so happy. They came so close that then we got afraid that we could get caught in their waves. My father always put a white flash, a message, and it said, "If you want to pick us up, we come close. If no, we stay away."

Some of the ships said, "Yes, we take you," and then when we came close, they tried to hit us to make us drown and die in the sea. My father knew they used that trick a lot. They didn't want us there, and if we died, nobody knew. So many people were coming out of Vietnam. Other countries didn't want to take any more. It's even worse today.

We go and go and go. In two weeks we saw a ship from Germany with a red cross on it. My father rowed, rowed, rowed and he came very nicely right next to the ship. The Germans took us on board their ship. They gave us food, a shower, blankets. They told us to sleep. And they asked to speak to the captain of the boat. My father, he doesn't know German but he knows French, he went and spoke French to them. They said, "Tomorrow we will take you and your people to an island, to a refugee camp."

My father said, "Oh, thank you very much."

―――――

The first island they brought us to was one where nobody had lived. It was called Coocoo. The food was poison, the water polluted. And the mosquitoes! People had come there, cut down the trees, and built some houses. But it was dangerous for the people and a lot of us were sick. Some of us died. They took us to the hospital at the refugee camp. They gave us injections.

After a month we had an interview from the United Nations. They called our names. My father said, "I worked for the United States government in South Vietnam." They took all the information down and then said, "Okay, we will call Washington, D.C. You must wait while we do that."

While we waited, my father worked for the chief commander in the refugee camp in Indonesia. I worked, too. The United Nations had donated some money to build some more houses to make the camp bigger. I sought them out for a job. They said, "If you want to help the people, gather the wood so they can build the barracks."

I said, "Fine, fine, I volunteer."

Most of the people at the refugee camp were Vietnamese. Some of them had so sad stories, oh my. "In Thailand they stole my sister," one said. "My brother and my mother got killed because the boat sink," another said. But on the island, we all lived together in barracks and life at that time was beautiful. Each day the United Nations gave every person a half cup of rice and a half cup of another food. The American Peace Corps came there, too. We people built a school and they tried to teach a little English. We stayed there for eight months until one afternoon we heard our name called again. They told us, "You have a sponsor from the United States."

I thought, Oh wow! A new land! A new life! The United Nations had a special boat to Singapore. They take the refugees that are leaving to that city, we stay a week, and from there we take an airplane to Hong Kong and on to Alaska.

———

I looked out the window of the airplane in Alaska and I was so surprised. I tell my father, "Rice! Rice! Rice is falling from the sky!" He explained to me what is snow. From there we went to California, where we stayed in a shelter for a week. The people said, "Enjoy this, soon you will be in your new home, Detroit, and there the weather is very cold."

It was January when we came to Detroit. I said, "What a dirty city." There were a lot of newspapers flying in the air, and it was so cold. A lady met us at the airport and took us in a really strange and crazy hotel filled with new immigrants and mental people. She said, "Here is fifty dollars. I'll see you in fifteen days." We never saw her again.

At night at the hotel, the people screamed loud. They banged on the walls. We had nothing to cook. We didn't know what to eat. We didn't know what is American food. My father went out to the corner store and he got some coffee and a sandwich. Then he bought some soup and some rice to cook. He told me, "Stay inside," I said, "Why? American people very nice. They wouldn't hurt anybody." He told me, "Stay inside."

I think of South Vietnam. It is a beautiful country. I think of my mother and brothers and sisters and grandmother. I think new people to America are hungry for their countries. Governments can be so cruel.

———

After two, three weeks, we had a phone call, a Vietnamese voice. We were excited. There were no other

Vietnamese in the hotel. He said, "You will meet your sponsor. It is a rabbi and his congregation. They have found a home for you. One of the ladies speaks French, so you can talk to them."

When we meet them, the lady asks me, "Von, do you drink milk?" I'm too big to drink milk. With Vietnamese, milk is only for a baby. It is too expensive to buy.

I think, this is strange. Why does she ask me this?

"How about soda?" she says.

"Oh, yes, I love soda."

"What kind of food do you eat? Hamburger?"

I tell her, "Oh, I love hamburger." I never eat hamburger, but I'd heard of it a lot.

So they took us to our home. It was in the basement, one bedroom and one living room. The Jewish people from the temple, everybody gave a little bit. We got a TV, two beds, some furniture, a table, cups and plates and cooking things. After that the lady and the rabbi took us to a supermarket. They said, "Von, take all the food you want."

I had never seen anything like this supermarket. The lady showed me the shopping cart and what to do. The first thing I grabbed was Coca-Cola. I knew that. And bread. Then I looked around and I didn't see anything to eat. It was all frozen. I'd never seen that in Vietnam. There we had all fresh fruit and vegetables. I got some cans of food. At the refugee camp, I saw those for the first time.

The lady said, "Do you like potato chips?"

I said, "What are potato chips?"

She bought some chicken for us. My father said, "I feel so bad. They brought us here and they had to take us shopping." That afternoon, three more Jewish ladies came to the house. They showed us how to cook, how to make chicken, how to use the stove, where to put the milk and soda. They were so nice. I didn't understand a word they said, but I always smiled.

The next day they took me and my father shopping for clothes. I was so skinny and the pants were so big. They told my father and me, "You have to come to temple to meet the people." I got shoes, too. They said to my father, "Tomorrow, we will take Von to get a shot so you can put him in school."

They got my father a job as a typewriter repairman. He didn't know anything about that. He wanted to work on the ships, but they said to do that you must be a United States citizen. He said, "Okay."

I was very scared to start school after six years. I had to skip a lot of grades. Most of the students looked at me because the way I was dressing was strange. It was so cold, I wore everything I'd bought. I didn't know where anything was. I came late to every class. I was confused and I could not ask people. They told me in sign language, "Go to eat." I went into the cafeteria. There were hundreds of people.

———

A supervisor knew I was a new student. He took me to the head of the line to get a hamburger and the other students got angry. "Why does that boy get to go first?" I told the supervisor, "I want to wait in the line. Please." He said, "Don't worry about it. Take the food."

On that day and on other days, when I had a hard problem to solve, or when I felt sad or confused, I always look back on my past. I say, "Wow, what happened in the past is even harder. This is nothing." Let's face it, this is easy here.

There were no Vietnamese kids at the school, and only one Chinese boy, but he became my best friend. After a while I got along with the other students. I met a very nice black boy. He thought I was Chinese and all Chinese know karate and kung fu. He said, "I like your country's movies." I told him, "I'm Vietnamese." But he didn't know what was Vietnamese. He took me home to meet his mother and, wow, did they have a big TV. He said, "What do you want? Food?" "Yeah." He made food for me and we ate and drank soda. I didn't understand what I was seeing. I couldn't answer his questions, but we understood each other.

Later I invited him to my house. I was doing the laundry, but I didn't know how to do laundry here. In Vietnam we use a brush to scrub it, then take it outside and hang it in the wind. I washed it by hand in the bathtub and left it to dry. Two, three days, and it was not dry! The boy went, "Von, what is this? Why don't you bring it to a laundromat?" He didn't know my family never had even seen a washing machine.

Other kids did bring some trouble to me. They talked about the way my hair looked, my clothes. When they called me "Chinese," they did it to make fun of me. They didn't call me by name. They laughed because I could not speak well. I was really upset about it, but then again I thought, so what?

I took an art class and the teacher said, "You draw whatever you like." I drew a map of Vietnam, the boat I escaped in, my family, and all the blood. One of my drawings I put in my father's bedroom and on it I wrote, "NO MORE WAR!!!"

I got along well with my teachers. The English teacher gave me vocabulary to learn, like "breakfast," "dinner," "orange juice." I'd take it home and translate and study it. The pronunciation was hard for me, words like "brother." I'd practice my English by recording my voice on a tape recorder. I'd read from a book, then play it back. I watched TV news a lot, CNN.

———

Even though my father was working, the rabbi paid the rent, the telephone bill, the food, everything for six months! They took us to the temple and made a party to introduce us. They gave us a hat to wear, a yamulka. We still have it today. They knew it was my birthday. I had never had a birthday party in my life. They made a big cake and they told me to hold it and blow out the candles. They told me to give a speech. I was only here two, three months. I didn't know anything. My father said, "Whatever people give you, you have to say 'thank you.' " I said, "Thank you, thank you."

It was wonderful. They gave me the whole cake to take home. I ate it for one month! Every day after school, I cut one piece and ate it. The rabbi always called to see how we were. He said, "If you have any problem, we are here to help."

After six months, I said to my father and the rabbi, "Let me go look for a job." We don't want the temple to pay for us any more.

The rabbi said, "We wouldn't recommend that you work. You better concentrate on school."

Without telling them, I looked. I saw a lot of students go to work, so I copied them. I started walking from my house. I went into a supermarket. I was interviewed by the manager and he told me, "Sorry, you have an English problem. Study more and come back in six months." I went into many supermarkets that day, many small stores.

They didn't understand what I was talking about. I didn't understand what I was talking about. But I already knew the words for juice, milk, fruit, so that's why I was interested in those stores. I went home. I was so sad. I didn't want to bother my father. He was very busy, too, learning a new job and studying English in night school.

The next day after school, I went to look again. My school had a work-study program and a teacher told me about a job at Burger King. I was interviewed and the boss knew that I had an English problem. I begged him, "I can do anything! I can take the cooking test, but I can't take the writing test. I don't know English." So he went check, check, check, like that, on the test and I passed. So my first job in America was to cook hamburgers. I took the frozen hamburger and put it inside the fire. That's all he wanted me to do.

But then I saw customers who didn't throw their food in the trash. I came out and I cleaned the tables. I saw someone had thrown sodas on the floor. I took a mop and cleaned it up. I wanted to show him that I could work. He gave me a uniform and said, "You start today."

I ran home and said to my father, "I must write a letter to the rabbi. I must say, 'Thank you for everything you've done for us. Someday when I have a good job, I will donate money to this temple to keep it forever. Now my father and I both work and won't need any more help.' "

My father said, "Oh, that is great."

The rabbi called my house. He said, "Von, we want to help you. We don't want anything from you. You've only been here a few months. Remember your school-work, but you do what you want." I sent my money to my mother.

———

My father and I have been here for a long time now, eight, nine years. For five years we have had all the papers in order to have my mother and my brothers and my sisters come here. We have sent a letter to the United States ambassador to Thailand. We have written to the United States representative at the United Nations. We contacted our congressman and he wrote a letter. The congressman said, "Your family is qualified to come to the United States. They are at the top of the list." Still we wait and we wait and we wait. The Communist government doesn't want to give them visas.

This year on July 4th my father and I became citizens of the United States. I'm a free man! I read the Constitution. We the people are all equal. Now no one can say, if the United States someday has a problem, "You have to go back to Vietnam." I love this country. This country is my country now. I never go back.

My brothers and sisters don't have the opportunities that I do. Today it is September and I am starting university. I am a very lucky person. And when my family gets here and we are together again, we will make such a celebration!

Source Notes

1. *New Voices: Immigrant Students in U.S. Public Schools* (Boston: National Coalition of Advocates for Students Publication, 1988), p. 11.

2. *Ibid.*, p. 12. According to 1980 statistics, if you include children whose parents were born in Puerto Rico, almost half the New York City schools' total enrollment came from families where the native language was not English.

3. Population Reference Bureau, Inc. 1988. The remaining immigrants classified as "other." The figures are as follows:

   1861–1900, 68 percent north and west Europe, 22 percent south and east Europe, 7 percent North America, 2 percent Asia

   1901–1920, 41 percent north and west Europe, 44 percent south and east Europe, 6 percent North America, 4 percent Asia, 4 percent Latin America

   1921–1960, 38 percent north and west Europe, 20 percent south and east Europe, 19 percent North America, 18 percent Latin America, 4 percent Asia

   1961–1970, 39 percent Latin America, 18 percent north and west Europe, 15 percent south and east Europe, 13 percent Asia, 12 percent North America

1971–1980, 40 percent Latin America, 35 percent Asia, 11 percent south and east Europe, 7 percent north and west Europe, 4 percent North America

1981–1985, 48 percent Asia, 35 percent Latin America, 6 percent south and east Europe, 5 percent north and west Europe, 2 percent North America

4. *Ibid.*

5. Key immigration legislation includes:

   1882—temporarily barred Chinese immigrants

   1886—barred convicts, the insane, the severely retarded, and people likely to need public care

   1902—permanently barred Chinese immigrants

   1907—Japan agreed to stop Japanese laborers from coming to U.S.

   1917—adult immigrants were required to prove they could read and write at least one language

   1917—barred most Asian and Pacific islands immigrants

   1921—quotas established, limiting the total number of immigrants to 3 percent of that nationality's percent of the U.S. population in 1910, blacks and Asians excluded

   1924—"national-origin system" quotas revised, limiting the total number of immigrants based on that nationality's percent of the U.S. population in 1920, blacks and Asians excluded

   1943—exclusion of Chinese immigrants discontinued

   1952— maintained the "national-origins system," but set quotas for nations that had been excluded

   1965—amended law with one quota for Western Hemisphere, one quota for Eastern Hemisphere

6. According to a nationwide survey conducted by a *Los Angeles Times* poll and reported 9/19/88, U.S.-born citizens continue to be hostile and unwelcoming to immigrants. A majority, 64 percent, of those polled think that immigrants take more than they give to the country.

7. Immigration and Naturalization Service, Statistical Analysis, 1987.

8. *Ibid.*, 1988. The remaining five countries with the highest number of refugees coming to the U.S. were Czechoslovakia, Cambodia, Poland, Rumania, and Vietnam.

Bibliography

BOOKS

Allen, James Paul and Eugene Taylor. *We the People: An Atlas of America's Ethnic Diversity.* New York: Macmillan, 1988. (Adult)

Althen, Gary. *American Ways: A Guide for Foreigners in the United States.* Yarmouth, Maine: Intercultural Press, 1988. (A)

Anderson, Lydia. *Immigration.* New York: Franklin Watts, 1981. (Young Adult)

Ashabranner, Brent. *The New Americans: Changing Patterns in U.S. Immigration.* New York: Dodd, Mead & Co., 1983. (YA)

Axelrod, J.A. *Counseling and Development in a Multicultural Society.* Monterey, CA: Brooks/Cole, 1985. (A)

Blumenthal, Shirley. *Coming to America: Immigrants from Eastern Europe.* New York: Delacorte Press, 1980. (YA)

Blumenthal, Shirley and Jerome S. Ozer. *Coming to America: Immigrants from the British Isles.* New York: Delacorte Press, 1981. (YA)

Bouvier, Leon F. *Think about Immigration: Social Diversity in the U.S.* New York: Walker & Co., 1988. (YA)

Briggs, Vernon M., Jr. *Immigration Policy and the American Labor Force.* Baltimore: Johns Hopkins University Press, 1984. (A)

Edwards, Gabrielle I. *Coping with Discrimination.* New York: The Rosen Publishing Group, Inc., 1986. (YA)

Garver, Susan and Paula McGuire. *Coming to America: Immigrants from Mexico, Cuba and Puerto Rico.* New York: Delacorte Press, 1981. (YA)

Kismaric, Carole. *Forced Out: The Agony of the Refugee in Our Time.* New York: Random House, 1989. (A)

Lamm, Richard D. and Gary Imhoff. *The Immigration Time Bomb.* New York: Dutton, 1985. (A)

Lanier, Alison R. *Living in the U.S.A.* Yarmouth, Maine: Intercultural Press, revised 1988. (A)

Meltzer, Milton. *Taking Root: Jewish Immigrants in America.* New York: Farrar, Straus & Giroux, 1976. (YA)

Orfalea, Gregory. *Before the Flames: A Quest for the History of Arab Americans.* Austin, Texas: University of Texas Press, 1988. (A)

Pascoe, Elaine. *Issues in American History: Racial Prejudice.* New York: Franklin Watts, 1985. (YA)

Pedersen, Paul. *Handbook for Developing Multicultural Awareness.* Alexandria, Virginia: American Association for Counseling and Development, 1988. (A)

Perrin, Linda. *Coming to America: Immigrants from the Far East.* New York: Delacorte Press, 1980. (YA)

Reimers, David M. *The Golden Door: The Third World Comes to America.* New York: Columbia University Press, 1985. (A)

Rips, Gladys Nadler. *Coming to America: Immigrants from Southern Europe.* New York: Delacorte Press, 1980. (YA)

Robbins, Albert. *Coming to America: Immigrants from Northern Europe.* New York: Delacorte Press, 1980. (YA)

Spielberger, C.D. and R. Diaz-Guerrero, editors. *Cross-Cultural Anxiety.* Washington, D.C.: Hemisphere, 1986. (A)

Stone, Scott and John McGowan. *Wrapped in the Wind's Shawl: Refugees of Southeast Asia and the Western World.* San Rafael, CA: Presidio Press, 1980. (YA)

Tax, Meredith. *Union Square.* New York: William Morrow & Co., 1988. (A)

Weyr, Thomas. *Hispanic U.S.A.: Breaking the Melting Pot.* New York: Harper & Row, 1988. (A)

BOOKLETS

National Coalition of Advocates for Students Research and Policy Report. *New Voices: Immigrant Students in U.S. Public Schools.* Boston, MA., 1988. (single copy, prepaid price for schools, libraries, and other institutions: $12.95. Order from NCAS, 100 Boylston Street, Suite 737, Boston, MA 02116) (A)

The Commission on Minority Participation in Education and American Life, A Report. *One-Third of a Nation.* Washington, D.C., American Council on Education, Education Commission of the States. (A)

About the Author

For more than a dozen years, Janet Bode has worked as a free-lance writer. During this time, she has had five nonfiction books published. *View from Another Closet* and *Fighting Back* were for adults.

The other three were Franklin Watts young adult publications. *Rape: Preventing It; Coping with the Medical, Legal, and Emotional Aftermath* was chosen by the National Council for Social Studies for its award, Outstanding Social Studies Book. *Kids Having Kids: The Unwed Teenage Parent* was cited by the American Library Association in its category Best Books for Young Adults. Her latest book is *Different Worlds: Interracial and Cross-Cultural Dating*.

Ms. Bode's work also appears regularly in many national periodicals where she covers a wide range of controversial topics from "Love at First Sight" in *Glamour* to "Cocaine Addiction" in *Mademoiselle*. In addition, she collaborates on projects with cartoonist Stan Mack, including an upcoming humor-mystery-adventure-graphic novel.

Ms. Bode has lived and worked not only in the United States, but also in Europe and Mexico. She now resides in New York City, where she is a member of the Authors Guild and the National Writers Union.